Explore. Engage.

PLOT *twist*

MARK SEPHTON

First Printing 2016

ISBN-13: 978-1541140158
ISBN-10: 154114015X

Edited by Meredith Pruden - www.meredithpruden.com
Cover and Layout by Heather Westbrook - www.hwdesigns.info

CONTENTS

Foreword

FOREWORD

Behind every book is a story. This one is no different. The name *Plot Twist* came on my final day in Austin, Texas after spending two weeks there during SXSW— an event celebrating innovation, film and music. I was out exploring with some friends when the plans we'd set for the afternoon came to a grinding halt. We had decided to go and explore Barton Springs. It was a glorious, sunny day, and we had a couple of hours set aside with limited time. When we arrived at the springs, the National Park attendant informed us it was extremely popular that day, and they were operating a one car in and one car out policy. We'd have to wait an hour before we could park up. I was disappointed, as my friends had been building up my expectation by sharing how amazing and beautiful this place was. Before I could dwell on the disappointment, my friend in the back seat shouted, "Plot twist." I said to her, "What do you mean? Explain what you mean." She explained that when she and her friends' plans get changed or cancelled, instead of getting frustrated or disappointed, they shout "Plot twist" to recognise that while they may not like that what they'd set out to do is no longer available, they would focus their energy and excitement on exploring a new unknown adventure. In that moment, the words "plot twist" echoed in my ears, and I found myself quickly shifting from disappointment into excitement. It did something to me.

I like when things do something to me— a little nugget, a simple mindset shift, changed my outlook. I had been thinking about a title for my next book, and there was no way I was going to go with *Inside Job 2*. I believe, just like the name you give a child or the name you give a business, there is power in the name.

Calling this book *Plot Twist* embodies the premise of what it's about— that we all have a story to tell. We all have plans and agendas. Yet, things don't always go to plan and, sometimes, things come from left field to take us in another direction. This book is about equipping you and challenging you to embrace adventure rather than dwelling in disappointment (losing time and energy on things that don't matter) by constantly working on yourself and your mind.

Like my first book, *Inside Job*, this book is about developing you— the way you think and operate. It's about storytelling and imparting real strategies that are effective. Stories are the best way to communicate with people. We all want something with which to relate. We want to take knowledge and apply it to action.

Time to write again and explore all that's within me. Writing *Inside Job* created a huge wave of curiosity in who I am and, in particular, some of my unorthodox methods. During my book launch, people asked if I had plans to write another book. At that point, I didn't. I literally hadn't any other thoughts or feelings left in my brain to write down on paper, such was the expression of my own journey of personal development. I emptied my mind of all the blueprints, strategies, tips, tricks, habits, behaviours, thoughts and feelings for personal and professional development into *Inside Job*. Nearly 18 months have passed since that time. As I sit here today, I realise that a big part of me in these last months has been about experiencing and living life to again write something of value.

Unlike *Inside Job*, where I had the title before the content, this time around I am not even sure where this book will lead me— let alone you. Stay with me. I haven't wasted my time writing this for you to waste time and money reading it.

I like to write from the here and now expressing my thoughts through storytelling, as well as what whispers I hear in the world of entrepreneurship and personal development. I like to share my challenges in the hope they will resonate with you. I received countless letters and messages from people who read *Inside Job* expressing a feeling I'd written not just my life story but theirs. Somehow, I had gotten inside their brain and revealed personal stories of setbacks, trials and disappointments. The greatest books are the ones that are revealing and vulnerable but also full of actionable steps to improve lives and businesses.

Writing is a great way to release anxiety, stress and concerns. It feels like therapy. It's not often I feel anxious and, in all honesty, when I do I'm not always sure why. I believe we must give ourselves the best chance at success, and being proactive to life's curve balls helps us stay immune to some of the challenges and conflicts life throws at us. Writing helps to expel feelings of anxiety. When I write regularly, those feelings of anxiety rarely rear their heads at all. Similarly, if you suffer with depression, being proactive by taking care of how much you sleep, what you eat, with whom you spend time, going outside to enjoy the sun (or clouds) and keeping a gratitude diary will give you a foundation for reducing a depressive state of mind. We must do all we can to give ourselves the greatest chance of success.

In my book *Inside Job*, I go through action points to really stimulate gratitude and build a mindset that will keep you focused and moving forward despite the distractions and pressure we all face. I don't want you to just survive. I want you to flourish. I want your life to represent something of depth and influence.

The whole world, and everyone in it, is after our minds and full of distractions. Within only 30 minutes of writing, I've had several distractions— mostly Tweets, emails, texts and phone calls. Everyone wants a piece of you.

PLOT *twist*

CHAPTER I

RELATIONSHIPS

"The business of business is relationships;
The business of life is human connection."
– Robin S. Sharma

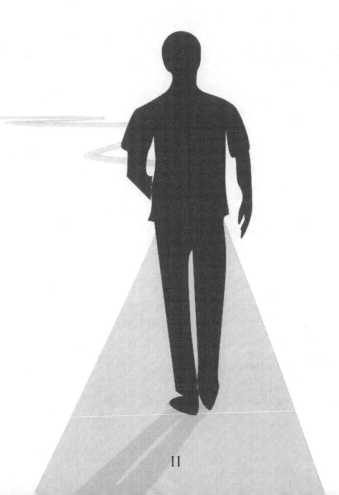

We forge countless relationships through a lifetime. People come, and people go. When we travel and explore this world and all its beauty, it's often the people we come across that leave us with a hugely positive impression. Many individuals make an impression on me each time I travel.

While I was in Austin, it was amazing to see the new friendships I made and to experience the SXSW vibe was a huge eye opener. The power of social media has enabled me to build some really solid and exciting relationships with the most fascinating entrepreneurial minds of our time. I see Austin as a hotbed of entrepreneurship with a vibrant attitude toward personal growth and business. SXSW is no different with its mix of entrepreneurship, music and innovation. It really left me with abundant amounts of creativity and opportunity.

I bang the drum about the power of meaningful relationships all the time— the need to invest in people, get to know them and listen to them. Your ability to listen is your greatest gift. My trip to SXSW stemmed from my ability to communicate and be social. My ability to build meaningful relationships with those who strike a cord with my purpose and energy has cultivated an authentic and organic community of likeminded people around whom I enjoy being.

I acknowledge my own personal struggles with travelling to various destinations. I can't say I enjoy travelling. I like arriving at my destination without the uncertainty of flights, issues with baggage, customs and immigration. Throw into this experience the fact I'll be away from my three beautiful children whom I've never been apart for more than a day, and you have an unsettled man.

I have just found a handwritten note from my eldest daughter in my bag. I'm now on board my flight to Austin. Her letter has energised me, and I am ready for the adventure ahead. Thankfully, I've passed through the various checks and am settled into my seat. I strategically picked a seat where I believed nobody would be sitting directly next to me, and I guess I lucked out. The man closest to me heads a division of one of the largest computer gaming companies in the world. We are both thankful for the vacant seat between us. Despite being glad for the extra space, I will speak with anyone. However, it's always nice to build a rapport with someone who is fascinated with your work and philosophy and vice versa. We exchanged contact details quickly. Who knows where such a connection will take us. I really encourage you to look up and engage with the world around you. We were called to build a vibrant and self-sustaining community. I get a kick out of meeting new people and always have prided myself on my network. This new connection also has helped me relax and not feel so isolated and vulnerable as I travel.

It is amazing what people can accomplish when they travel on an airplane. For me, it was about engaging with those around me, but for others it's really about getting work done.

The inspiration for this chapter is a recent interview with one of my favourite authors, Daniel Priestley, about the process he uses when writing a new book. He told me he writes 70 percent of his books on long-haul flights. Daniel has a base in Shanghai and writes from the moment the seatbelt sign goes off until the battery on his laptop dies. His style is certainly very different from mine. When I wrote *Inside Job*, I wrote it within a six-month period writing 30 minutes a day Monday through Friday with weekends off. It worked for me, but I liked the challenge of writing for a longer period to see if it's for me.

It's important to try new ways of doing things even if you've had success with other ways in the past. You learn more about yourself and the process. But, as with anything, it has to work for you. If the process you use isn't resonating with your style, it's wise to find a different way or, perhaps, a way you already know brings about the desired result. If I reflect on my own style, my personality and strengths lend themselves to short, intense bursts of high energy. It makes sense that I write for short periods of highly focused intensity when the words seem to flow out of me. Long periods of focus leave me tired and unable to articulate my own thoughts.

During one of my more recent *Inside Job* Mastermind Groups, I carved out a section where I shared my own skills, stories and strategies in building and cultivating meaningful relationships. I've already shared how relationships can be formed through social media and can stimulate some of the most incredible opportunities and experiences of your life when honoured and nurtured. But, how do you build these meaningful relationships? If you start to faithfully invest in and make room for the following key attributes, you'll see an increase in your influence and in your ability to positively impact relationships— not just in business but in every area of your life.

Action points

How to cultivate super positive relationships

1. **Give first.** Lead from the front. Be the first to give. Instigate conversation, and build a rapport. Have the courage to take the first step. When I've initiated and looked to serve those around me, whether strangers or dear friends, it's made a difference— even if very small. Take your eyes off yourself to set the giving standard.

2. **Pay attention to detail.** If we want to be held in high regard and really impact those around us, our ability to pay attention to details is critical. Last year, I nearly lost a friendship because I forgot their birthday. It was never my intention and, to a degree, I thought they were overreacting, but we moved on. I don't bring this up to cause another problem but to be real and acknowledge my own human side. I pride myself on my network, and one of my daily habits is to wish everyone within it a happy birthday. On this occasion, I missed a birthday and the friend was miffed. They'd seen me send countless others best wishes yet, when it came to this person, I'd well and truly messed up. It was an easy mistake to make. I was juggling lots of balls at the time and, on this occasion, I dropped one. This is just one detail that can harm your relationships. Pay attention to what your network is doing personally and professionally. Ask them questions about their adventures to really make a positive impact. I take time to check in on all my close contacts as a point of priority as often as I can. Maya Angelou said, "People may not remember what you did, but they will always remember how you made them feel." Detail is key! How can you be creative and thoughtful in your network?

3. **Make time.** I have a couple of really key relationships with people in my inner circle. I have a weekly commitment to invest in these relationships and take intentional time to prioritise them. They are my VIPs. We all need a core group of friends in whom we can invest but equally inspire us to grow and develop. Children spell the word love "T-I-M-E." It's no different for adults. We need to be strategic about to whom we give our time. I am a firm believer of not casting our pearls before swine. We need to be mindful that some of the people in whom we invest are not actually deserving of the time or good stewards

of the attention we give. We can't afford to spend precious energy on those who are unappreciative. It's worth it to seek out those who value what you offer and authentically reciprocate your positive nature by taking time to listen and enjoy your company too. We don't get to pick our family, but we do get to pick our friends and we must choose wisely. The important thing is to invest in people who appreciate and respect our time. These are the very people we need to be giving the best of ourselves. We need to create a healthy and vibrant community that helps nourish each other's minds, souls and spirits. I realise your circle actually becomes smaller as your success grows and you gain clarity in your purpose. That's why due diligence is needed when creating and investing in your inner circle. This viewpoint isn't about being selfish but about taking care of your mental health to create the life you want and protect your time and energy for the people who deserve your attention.

4. **Listen.** The greatest gift you can give someone is to listen. Why? Because the world claims our time and, most importantly, our minds. We are so distracted. When we truly listen and take time to pay attention to what someone is saying without our mind drifting, it impacts people in a huge way. I met with a prospective client about six months ago. We met for a coffee to determine if I was the right mentor for her and if she was the right client for me. I listened to her for 30 minutes straight without interruption— without once looking at my phone or thinking about what I was having for dinner. After she finished talking, she looked me in the eye and said, "Mark, I have not been listened to like this in years." I said, "Fabulous, I've not listened to anyone like that in years." She became my client, and I've since seen this woman grow personally and professionally. Listening to who she was, what she wanted and what she needed, allowed me to

serve her in a way that helped develop her greatest strengths. If we listen to people, they often will lead with what they want and need. It's amazing how so few are listening but, instead, are hellbent on selling an idea or product that they love but their customer does not. We need to get out of our own way, be quiet and switch on in the right moment.

5.   **Followthrough.** A lack of followthrough has broken my trust and respect in people more than anything else. I am a reasonable and gracious man if the situation and circumstances warrant it. However, when people move the goal posts, it grates on me. If I commit to something, I'm all in regardless of how I feel or if it's going to cost me something. One of the main reasons people dislike networking is because of the lack of followthrough. It's easy to promise but harder to deliver. In the end, it is much better not to commit to something than to commit and pull out. It costs you not just in business but in your personal relationships too. Nobody can trust you if you're constantly changing your mind or backing out of obligations. Changing your mind mid-stream or without good reason is no way to conduct yourself or your business. Be a person of your word.

6.   **Serve.** Proactively help a key relationship once a month. Once you've identified a person in whom you want to invest, start serving them. Help them get what they want. Give the very best of your time and resources without expecting anything back or having an agenda. Look for ways to bless others. The whole premise of servant-leadership is to like people enough to see them succeed and grow through the gift of our tools, resources, mistakes, failings and successes.

7.   **Be transparent.** I find transparency to be so liberating. When we're real, it liberates others to be vulnerable.

When it comes to being vulnerable, it must be coupled with wisdom in order to serve you and not result in heartache. Don't just show everyone your best side. Instead, show them the real you— that, like everyone else, you are on a journey. When we communicate who we are without fear of judgment, we connect, engage and impact on all those within our sphere of influence. It helps to show on what we're working and with what we're struggling. No one likes to be sold text book answers and predictable ways of doing things. It's the human condition to desire fresh and honest engagement. Show people your motivation through clear action and communication.

8. **Be kind.** To some, kindness is interpreted as weakness. I remember when business people built reputations by doing whatever it took to succeed— even manipulating, bullying and abusing others to fulfil their own ambitions. People like that are not the people with whom I work or spend time. I've made progress in my personal and professional life by being kind, courteous and knowing when to admit wrongdoing and ask forgiveness. When we think of others first, it improves our own mental health. He who refreshes others will be refreshed. Kind gestures of gratitude and thanks go a long way. Compliments and a genuine interest in another person's endeavours are statements that convey kindness.

9. **Be joyful.** Nobody wants to be around someone who is grumpy. Lacking joy makes you no fun to be around. Joy is based on what we know to be true, which really means that we are loved, that we are important and that our life has a purpose. Regardless of your occasional circumstances where you may feel unhappy about something, you can still find joy in your current situation. There is a clear difference between joy and happiness. Happiness is based on

feelings. When things are going well in your life, you'll have high levels of happiness. But, why is it that some people are able to find joy despite experiencing the most difficult and stressful situations in their lives? It's simple really. They choose to focus on the positive and what is true in whom they are rather than on what they currently feel because of a given situation. We need to allow joy to govern and guide us. When we do, we bring greater opportunity through positive choices even as we weather the occasional storm.

10. **Be honourable.** I love what honour does to a person. It can lift someone's spirit. It can increase their sense of value. It can give wings to the human soul. It continues to be a dying art form but, when tapped into, can have magnificent results. I recall two clear moments of this. I mentioned one in *Inside Job*. When Joel Rodriguez met me at the airport, took my bags, gave me water and called me "Sir" though he'd only ever heard about me through a mutual friend. Ironically and excitedly, I'm seeing him in just a few days when he meets me in Austin. That act of honouring me has stuck with me and resulted in a life-long friendship, which I value dearly. Joel gets the best of me. I prioritise him because we are good for each other. The other moment happened only a few months ago. Something incredible happened to me and my business— a real proud moment. Sadly, many people don't like seeing others succeed let alone celebrate that success. However, one man recently did. His name is Gary, and he does so much for others and for the community at large. I hold him in very high regard because he is respectful and kind but, most of all, he knows how to honour others. When you do something well, he's the first to celebrate with you and help you tell the world. The way he speaks is uplifting and sincere. He puts others before himself. He shows high levels of appreciation and gratitude.

Because of the way he lives and acts, he will always have my attention, support and listening ear. These acts cost you nothing. All they take is your ability to see others and hold them in a higher regard than you do yourself. This is honourable behaviour.

11. **Practice forgiveness.** The power to forgive is not to be lost and is not just for the spiritual or religious. Everyone makes mistakes. We get things wrong. We say the wrong thing. But, it's vitally important we allow the bigger picture of someone's innate personality to form our opinion of them. When you know someone's true heart and character, you can overlook simple lapses in judgment and respond graciously to mishaps. We all need to issue forgiveness to those around us. Forgiveness is for our own benefit, freedom and personal growth. We can't expect people to walk on a tightrope— it's not fair. I'm constantly searching for higher guidance with this one too. There is a huge difference between forgiveness and forgetting. We shouldn't forget the times we've been hurt. Often, there are lessons to be learned. But, we should forgive those who get it wrong. That way, when we get it wrong too (and we will), we can be released from our mistakes and move on.

CHAPTER 2

FIND YOUR DAVID

"I define connection as the energy that exists between people when they feel seen, heard, and valued; when they can give and receive without judgment; and when they derive sustenance and strength from the relationship."
– Brené Brown

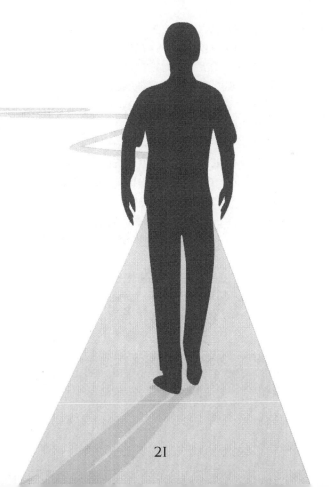

A lot happened during the two weeks I spent in Austin. What a great vibe and buzz during SXSW. I hit the city hard, networked my butt off and said "Yes" to every opportunity, which enabled me to increase my influence and share my story.

I'm on the flight back, in a reflective mood and thinking back on the things I did well and the things that didn't go so well. The mistakes I made and the success I cultivated. I'm thinking about the people I met and didn't meet. I ask myself several burning questions. Did I make an impact? Did I seize every opportunity? Did I uphold myself in class and sophistication. Is Austin richer for me having been there? Are its people richer for making my acquaintance?

Sometimes the answers to these types of questions are more challenging to swallow than the questions themselves. I tend to do what I want to do. So if I show up or make a decision to do something, good news, I will follow through and execute. Equally, trying to persuade me to do something for which I have no passion or desire is like asking a car to fly. What that means is I protect my energy by doing what I love and serving the people I want to serve. The challenge arises when everyone else has that same expectation of my time and attention.

I'm so passionate about relationships that it's no surprise where I tend to focus my reflections. My trip to Austin was to make deeper connections with those I'd already established a relationship— connections previously made through the unbelievable power of social media. But, one of the highlights of my trip was meeting a man called David. I'd never engaged with David before— not even on social media. We were complete strangers who just happened to be in the same space at the same time. Don't you just love those organic and authentic connections? I find they often produce a whole load of opportunities and excitement.

There's something incredible about coffee shops. I'd just finished speaking to the largest prosthetic limbs manufacturer in the United States about building synergy and creating change in a company culture. Afterward, I found this incredible independently-owned coffee shop with a great entrepreneurial and youthful vibe to it. It was a welcome haven to reflect on my talk and enjoy a latte. The place was buzzing with life and filled with lots of techies, writers, readers and entrepreneurs. I was in my element. Unfortunately, the popularity also meant limited seating and nowhere to plug in. I surveyed my surroundings and fixed my eyes on David. He was working and had his work spread over four seats and two tables.

As I approached David, our eyes met and I asked if there was room for me to charge my phone. He graciously obliged and began moving his work to make room. I thanked him and made myself comfortable. A mutual curiosity emerged. I was naturally drawn to what David was doing, and he was curious as to what an Englishman was doing in Austin. We connected on such a remarkable level that an instant rapport formed.

David recently had moved to the city to help launch a flagship store in the area. He was working hard on recruitment and marketing. We each shared what a normal day looked like in our lives and talked about what I do for a living. David showed a genuine interest in what I had to say. When he learned I was speaking a few days later, he booked himself and his wife into the event right there on the spot.

The things I most love about David are his energy, big smile, kind eyes and attentive nature. His body language was super positive, warm and open. We shared some of the individual paths we'd taken without fear of judgment. Sometimes, it takes years to cultivate relationships like this because the confidence to be vulnerable takes courage (more on that later). Yet, something about our connection gave us license to travel through years of personal history to a quick mutual respect and understanding for each other.

I often am caught up with connecting with people all over the planet via social media, so it was refreshing to impact, and be impacted by, someone face to face. Two complete strangers are now two good friends and allies who are excited to see what the future holds. All thanks to open eyes and a desire to make a connection.

Some of the stand-out memories of my Austin adventure flowed out of my organic and authentic relationship with David. In a world full of noise and distraction, we must look up and around to practice the art of cultivating new relationships. We must see the opportunities to converse. Every best friend, best client and best connection started as a stranger. This is a theme in my life.

David took me to some of the greatest shows, events and secret spots in Austin. He introduced me to his community, and I introduced him to mine. We collaborated, we served each other, we explored, we connected and we created memories that will serve me in years to come. There are Davids all around us. We just need to be willing, brave and confident in who we are and open our mouths to engage in conversations. My connection with David was one of the greatest first meetings of my life. It was a powerful reminder never to lose sight of opportunities to connect with the people we pass in daily life.

CHAPTER 3

PAY ATTENTION

"There is ecstasy in paying attention... Anyone who wants to can be surprised by the beauty or pain of the natural world, of the human mind and heart, and can try to capture just that— the details, the nuance, what is. If you start to look around, you will start to see."
– Anne Lamott

I have countless stories from my adventures in Austin. During the SXSW craze, I went to a number of networking events ranging from startups showcasing their latest invention to the typical relaxed environment where you chat about business and life over a breakfast taco and coffee.

During a morning networking event, two things happened I've never before experienced. I love hearing and experiencing new things. It blows open possibilities and self revelations when we experience things for the first time. The first thing was being told by two separate people who was the most important person in the room, dutifully pointing to the gentleman. I acknowledged the recommendations and cut a swath for the man in question. I didn't first explore why they believed he was the most important person in the room because I like to find out things like that for myself.

He was casually dressed, making him seem approachable. I introduced myself, and we engaged in conversation for a few minutes. We explored what each of us did for a living and, more importantly, why we do it. We built a fairly instant rapport. Turns out this guy owns the largest tech company in Austin. Regardless of this revelation, it was his ability to listen and engage without the slightest bit of arrogance that spoke to me about his class and integrity.

Whenever I'm out networking I always carry copies of my book with me and this was no exception. I shared the premise of Inside Job, and it struck a cord with the "most important man in the room."

"Mark, I love what you are about, and I love what this book stands for," he said. "I want a copy." I reached into my

26

pocket to grab a pen and write him a personal message on his new copy of my book.

As I was signing, he leaned in close and said "Mark, I actually don't have any cash on me." I told him, "No problem," and that he could wire the money through PayPal later. He agreed and told me I would have the money within two hours. Sure enough, I did receive the money within two hours (remember, followthrough is one of the best ways to cultivate meaningful relationships). This guy follows through. It's no wonder he's such a success!

I was selling my books for $15 a piece, but most people who bought it just gave me $20 and told me to keep the change. It's an unbelievably generous mindset in America that I love yet challenges me. When his money dropped into my PayPal account, I was expecting $15— maybe $20. Instead, in true generous form, there was $100 with a note attached reading, "Thanks for the book. Paid for a couple more. Please give them out as you go."

This is the second new experience I had witnessed. Such a kind, open-hearted gesture thrilled me, challenged me and raised the bar on my own ability to pay it forward, make a difference and use my own wealth to leave a positive impact.

To honour him and his gesture during the rest of my trip, I carefully considered people with whom I connected that I believed would most benefit from my book. I considered people who would love to read it but, perhaps, couldn't afford a copy. I was sensitive to each person I met. When I identified individuals who would benefit, I'd write the name of the man who owned the largest tech company in Austin as the gift giver and take a picture of the recipient. I sent the collection to him a few days after I'd returned to the United Kingdom.

Acts of kindness are a huge game changer for everyone. That's why it's so fun to give! I was blessed, the people who received the books were blessed to receive a free copy and the man who started paying it forward will be blessed by the time this book goes to print and he reads testimonies of his kind gesture. I salute you, sir.

CHAPTER 4

MAKE THINGS HAPPEN

"If you really want to do something, you'll find a way. If you don't, you'll find an excuse."
– Jim Rohn

During my time In Austin, I'd planned a small event where my contacts could come and hear me speak to engage with me on a deeper level beyond the realm of what's possible via social media.

It was incredible to see so many making the effort to attend one of my events. People traveled far and wide. It was mind blowing to see the connections and impressions I had made through social media that encouraged and convinced people they wanted to hear me speak and build a professional relationship. I don't mention this to make myself look good. I mention this because when we are motivated to do something, it's never a question of if but only how. When we are motivated toward a cause or reason, we make a plan and work that plan. When we know what is driving us, we are fully committed to making the opportunity a reality.

I'm always mindful that when I commit to something it's because I have the desire and passion to do it. When we really want to do something, we go after it with all our heart. We don't need convincing or to be persuaded because we're settled in our mind it's what we want to do.

We all have disappointment in our lives, but we must not stay there. It's not a place to dwell. I tend to get disappointed when people say they will do something and don't follow through with it. Alternatively, when people go above and beyond what I'd even be willing to do myself, it has a huge impact. This was no more evident than in Austin. I'd told all my contacts in the United States I was coming in the hope some of them would make plans to visit me.

One friend of mine did just that. The commitment and sacrifice he made to spend time with me was a powerful reminder of the old Rohn mantra, "If it's important to you,

you find a way. If not, you find an excuse." My friend lives in Montana— a good 26-hour drive from Austin. He made it happen in two days, travelling 16 hours the first day and another 10 hours the next day. Unbelievable.

I honestly think the most I've ever driven at once is six hours before I'm done. So, when Joel got in his car and traveled such long distances, it said a lot about his commitment to our friendship. When we are self-motivated, we make no excuses and, instead, take action and deliver. We are all motivated by something. When we know our motivation, we pull out all the stops. Regardless of the pain and sacrifice, we are willing to put in the work or take action to arrive at our destination.

It was great to connect and spend time with Joel. One thing I love about our friendship is that it creates the opportunity to engage with people. After a long day of networking with Joel playing chauffeur, we went out for food to kick back a little. From the moment he arrived in town, we spent the first few days networking our butts off. It was time for some rest and relaxation. We found this tavern and were reminiscing about years gone by. It's always incredible to look back on stories that feel like yesterday. It was a great evening of laughter and food.

In the midst of our evening, we were waited on by an incredibly creative woman, locals call only "Sheeba." She had a great energy. We all know we attract who we are (I talked about the law of attraction in *Inside Job*), and this experience was a living example of the law in motion. It was clear this woman was one of depth but had been through some challenging times. Sheeba had a spring in her step, she had character and she had my and Joel's curiosity.

After her shift, we met Sheeba for a drink to share our personal stories and how we ended up where we are. We're all where we are now because of the decisions we've made, and that can either look like a pretty picture or a train wreck. Either way, be encouraged because we can change our story and make the necessary changes to ensure we end up where we want. It was clear Sheeba has a naturally creative flair but needs the right opportunities and an understanding of the environments that bring out her best. The greatest opportunities are not out in the world. They are deep within you and must be cultivated.

Sheeba has her own fashion line and an uncanny ability to share stories through pictures and graphics. We all need a support network of people to rally around us and give us courage, knowledge and wisdom. Sheeba was at a crossroads in her life and began to make better choices about what she did and with whom she spent her time. Since that initial meeting, we've had several conversations to help her process and navigate through all the choices and decisions that lay in front of her. After experiencing some additional personal challenges, Sheeba decided it was in her best interest to go on a long road trip to explore the United States. She's still on the road, meeting new people, working remotely and exploring new opportunities. Sheeba's ability to change her environment to get clear with herself and prioritise her relationship with herself has served her well. We all have to make difficult decisions to move forward. I applaud Sheeba hitting the road to find out what is truly inside her. As Sheeba navigates through life searching her own heart, we all must do the same.

Steps to getting back on the right path:

- Take time out
- Listen to your heart
- Confide in those who love you, and ask them what they see in you
- Go on vacation, or take a road trip to get outside your own head
- Follow your gut, and follow the peace— the right path

always has a positive mix of excitement and peace
- Remember your WHY— don't lose sight of what you want your life to represent and for what you want to be remembered. Saying "Yes" to things that contradict your life's mission means you're heading in the wrong direction

CHAPTER 5

BUST YOUR CHOPS

*"The habit of doing more than is necessary can
only be earned through practice."*
—Seth Godin

After my 10-hour flight from London to Austin, I'd made plans to visit a spa to have a massage and release some of the stress and tension from travelling. In hindsight, I'm baffled why I've never scheduled myself a massage after a long-haul flight before. It was glorious. It was magical. It was exactly what I needed.

Back home, I have regular massages every other week, but I don't think I've ever appreciated one as much as I did that day. In some ways, I certainly received more than expected. I always ask the same question any place I get a massage for the first time. "What is the etiquette for a massage," I inquired. The gentleman replied, "Strip to your boxers." This is standard, so I stripped to my skivvies.

I was laying on my stomach ready for the therapist to join me in the room, feeling really good to just be lying down. My tummy was full of the pad Thai I'd eaten just before. I'd been starving! Tiredness and hunger are like a time bomb of anger and grumpiness for me, so I had to eat. I'm laying down on my front when I hear the door open and the therapist walk in. It's a beautiful room and a very relaxing environment. It's perfect for switching off. She lays two towels over my near naked body— one for my upper and one for my lower body. After about five minutes of her massaging me over these towels, she whips them off. She takes hold of my boxers and folds them into themselves so that two-thirds of my ass is revealed. This is fine, but blimey if you're going to fold them that much, you may as well have asked me to take them off in the first place. So, I'm lying on the bed with my ass practically out of my boxers, and she throws a towel over my head, mounting it with her knees on either side to apply hot oil to my back.

This was my first impression of Austin in a small place called China Town. The service was professional, the massage was phenomenal, the therapist just went places I wasn't expecting. But the experience was a very positive one because each team member was attentive and the vibe created the perfect ambiance. The combination created the tranquility needed to capture the rest and relaxation paramount to any good massage. When I arrived, I was greeted and given some water before being taken to a place where I could be still, breathe and relax. I was then given the option to choose where the massage would take place (either a private room or a more open space with very authentic and original Chinese tapestries). I find massage a fairly sacred experience, so I opted for the private room. After 90 minutes, the toil of travelling began to leave my body. The detail, care and attention to the music, the furnishings, the oil, the smells and the pressure of the therapist were picture perfect. After the massage, I was given green tea and 20 minutes to come around and get dressed. There was no sense of pressure or hurry. As I reflect back on the whole massage experience, a cheeky smile comes upon my face because the experience was memorable. If that was their goal, to provide a memorable service not just for the quality but for the specific detail to my body, then they succeeded. They did more than was necessary.

In today's world, our expectations have never before been so high. As we experience improved levels of service in some places, we naturally expect others to raise the bar too. Sadly, many businesses still don't deliver what we expect as a minimum— let alone exceed our expectations. This small, family run business achieved something that night. Foot Relax in Austin's China Town made a big enough impact for me to mention it here as a shining example of how to over deliver to your customer.

Another recent stand out moment for me was courtesy of Microsoft. Now, I normally like to give kudos to small businesses and find some of the bigger brands don't actually deliver high levels of service, but Microsoft totally bucked that trend. Their level of care in detail to correct a recent problem was top notch.

If you've ever owned a console, specifically an Xbox, you will know what the ring of death is. For those who don't, the ring of death is a sign your console is failing. Normally green when the device is turned on, the ring of death is a nickname for when the standby button turns red. I tried to fix it by turning the console on and off and resetting it, but nothing worked. I called Microsoft and answered a series of questions before the agent ascertained my Xbox would need to be checked by one of their engineers. They scheduled a courier to collect the console directly from my house and even organised a time and date convenient for me. When the courier arrived (right on time), he handed me a receipt and informed me Microsoft would respond within three days with an update and next steps. At this point, I had literally two days left on my 3-year warranty.

Rather than me waiting all three days, Microsoft actually called the next day to tell me the console was unrepairable. Before I could even be upset, the agent continued and told me they would be issuing a brand new one within four working days. Imagine my surprise when it arrived the very next day along with an apology and new warranty. As an added gesture, Microsoft also sent a free year pass to Xbox Live, which enables you to play on the Internet with other users. This service normally costs around £30 for a 12-month membership. The extra Xbox Live service may seem like no big deal, but Microsoft already had dealt with me in such a courteous and professional manner that this was just very tasty icing on the cake.

I long for businesses that are not just reactive but proactive toward service. Mistakes happen. Things die and need to be fixed. Sure, it can be frustrating, but it's a part of life. In this case, the overwhelming memory is not the death of my console but the company's ability to take responsibility, put it right and then go a little bit further with a few personal touches. The entire experience was so positive that I upgraded from the newly replaced Xbox 360 to an even newer Xbox One shortly after because I believe in the product and, most of all, in the service. I know, from firsthand experience, that I'm in good hands should something go wrong.

I have asked many times on radio, "What is the best piece of customer service you've ever been given?" What's sad is that most people can't name a single customer service experience that has blown them away. Here is one of the greatest opportunities knocking at the door of business owners. We need to be delivering such a high standard of service that our customers and clients become our sales force. When we get things right, people will share it from the rooftops. We know only too well that people like to complain via public forums, and it's often much more difficult to convince people to share positive experiences. This is just one reason why outstanding customer service is so important to your business. As an aside, it's also a great reason to be present on your social media channels to build connections with your customers and address issues as they arise.

CHAPTER 6

KEEP AUSTIN WEIRD

*"Small business isn't for the faint of heart. It's for the brave,
the patient and the persistent. It's for the overcomer."*
– Unknown

During a radio interview where local professor Red Wassenich was a guest, the phrase "Keep Austin Weird" was born through his message about promoting local entrepreneurship. A local, independent business panel subsequently adopted the phrase to encourage small business in the area. Red decided not to copyright the phrase, which then was adopted by numerous sources.

Austin is, in fact, a little weird, and that contributes to my overwhelmingly positive feelings toward the city. I love the people, the energy and the vibrancy of its businesses, shops and restaurants. There is a lot going on in Austin, and it certainly is an ideal place to do business and even set up a home. It is a totally different vibe to the other 12 states I've so far visited. At midnight, it is not strange to see people working out in a glass-fronted gym. Equally, I didn't see more than a handful of overweight people. On the flight over, the average age of the passengers was about 35 and there was no one who appeared to be over 45. It speaks of a very happening, vibrant and hip place. There is a huge tech scene and a forward-thinking mindset that embraces creatives and entrepreneurs who blaze their own trail. Some of the greatest businesses we are yet to experience will be birthed out of this city— mark my words.

Austin is a city that seems to embrace all within its borders. This was true of my experience. The place I stayed welcomed me with open arms. I was treated like family, given a key and encouraged to come and go as I pleased. The gift of hospitality is a beautiful one. When someone opens up their home, it speaks volumes of their generosity and ability to serve.

During SXSW, there were some of the most incredible music events going on. Thankfully, I managed to experience several. One particular event was taking place at the very first Whole Foods store, which was established here. Hundreds were gathered for this event. Bands from all over the country were performing on the rooftop. The sun was shining, and you could smell the Texas BBQ from down the street. It was a great atmosphere of music, chatter and fun. My friends arrived early and already were benefitting from the incredible music and tasty delights. I, on the other hand, had just joined the line waiting for admittance. I was told it would be a couple of hours before I would gain entry to the party, but I thought to myself, "That's okay." The sun was shining, I had a nice cold glass of lemonade, and I had no plans. Many of you who know me well know I typically like to dress in jeans with a nice shirt and a killer blazer. Despite the heat, this was no exception since I'd just finished a meeting with a potential client.

After about 15 minutes in the slow-moving line soaking up the rays, a young woman came up to me and started to engage in conversation. After chatting briefly, she handed me a credit card shaped VIP pass and explained the event is a three-day event but she can't attend the show that day. She continued by sharing how she believed I would appreciate this VIP pass. I was waiting for the sales pitch, but it didn't come. Instead, she said "Sir, I would like you to have it, and I would like you to enjoy yourself." I thanked her and she continued by informing me the VIP pass would give me certain privileges. All I needed to do was flash it at personnel to see the benefit. She said, "Great, you don't need to stay in line anymore. Just go right to the front, flash this pass, and they will let you straight up." I left the line, went straight to the front, flashed the pass and was guided up a flight of stairs. At the top, I was greeted by two men who offered me a drink and led me to the seating area where I could enjoy the bands and great food. It was a splendid day that perfectly represented the charm and appeal of such a generous city. While I am so grateful for the generosity this young lady showed me, I pondered why this stranger would single me out of the hundreds in line to give her VIP ticket. Many of us know when we do good to others it comes back, so I feel certain that's a part of it, but the second part is that I expect good and generous things to happen to me. But, there's more. When someone does right by me, I genuinely appreciate it and never forget it. Rightly or wrongly, I also believe it was how I was dressed. Don't let me lose you here. I just know from experience that how I dress does result in me being treated more favourably. I even was dubbed "fancy man" in Austin and seriously was treated like royalty with more attention and courtesy than I've ever been treated before when dressed for comfort. How you dress has an impact on how you are perceived. All these factors together made me stand out.

As it was SXSW, I was keen to check out as many events as I could while in town. I jumped onto Eventbrite and explored all the different events happening during my stay. I found about five events that sounded really good and like ideal places to find startups and entrepreneurs.

My buddy Joel came along to take in the experience, as he builds his film production company. Joel had booked onto the same events as me and, for most of my trip, was my set of wheels. I never like being late and would much rather be an hour early than even a second late. After lunch, we left downtown to head to the other side of the city, leaving plenty of time to make the event without any stress. Traffic was particularly bad, as it was the first day of SXSW. Regardless, we made good time and found a place to park just a short walk away from the venue. I jumped out of the car and walked over to the parking meter. It was $10 for a couple of hours, which I thought was pretty expensive but paid anyway. Would you believe the machine never printed me a parking ticket to display on the car dashboard. So, Joel called the number on the machine, and they assured us we wouldn't get booted.

We brushed ourselves off after this minor setback and walked over to the venue, which seemed awfully quiet. I took the escalator to where I believed the event was being held, and there was not a soul to be seen. I jumped back onto the Eventbrite app and realised the event was not being held at this location even though the business was hosting the event. Instead, it was being held at a place downtown only a block from where we had lunch! For a split second, that revelation went down like a lead balloon, but Joel started to laugh and that seemed like the only thing to do after experiencing all those obstacles. We must stop wasting energy on things we can't control. Another plot twist during my Austin trip, and a great opportunity to see the funny side instead of allowing frustration to linger for the rest of the evening. I quickly got the frustration out of my system and what transpired an hour after this was one of the highlights of my trip.

The event was all about startups showcasing their various businesses and concepts. The place was packed. We managed to speak with a number of startups and built a healthy network of people with whom to do business. One of the showcase businesses was an app built by a husband-wife team. The wife, Maria, had noticed I was carrying some books, and the cover caught her eye. She enquired, wanting to see it. She shared that she had seen the book before and asked if it was mine. When I informed her it was, in fact, my book, she excitedly said she wanted a signed copy. I enquired about her excitement, and she shared how her professor in Arizona had been referencing from my book during a recent seminar. That was incredible to hear. It also serves as a reminder to never bemoan a day filled with obstacles. We spend hours as entrepreneurs doing behind-the-scenes work that no one sees, but if you don't lose heart, stay consistent and measure action with results, things will start to take root and people will notice you.

It blew my mind that I could travel 4,000 miles from home and meet someone who had been directly impacted by my book. Paying $10 for parking didn't seem such a headache anymore. When things go wrong, dust yourself off, but don't stay in that negative energy. Get it out of your system, and go again. That night, I sold a bunch of books and made some great contacts. My ability to let go of the frustration and get my head in the game resulted in one of the stand-out moments of my whole experience in Austin.

Austin and its people impacted me in a positive way. I'm eager to return and revisit some significant connections in the world of entrepreneurship. It really is a little hot bed of culture, and my overall experiences were favourable. There was one disappointment I want to share as a reminder we must not only exceed customer expectations, we also must meet their basic wants and needs.

The U.S. has long been regarded as the flagship for customer service in the world. You can still experience great service when you visit this wonderful country. However, when I used to think of customer service, I would always think exclusively of my American colleagues and friends. Perhaps the rest of the world has caught up, or maybe things have changed a little based on what I have experienced during my more recent visits. Having worked in the hospitality industry for 10 years, I always appreciate great service and have a hard time accepting poor and inexcusable customer service.

We all occasionally have bad days. Perhaps a certain Colombian-style restaurant in Austin was having one of those bad days when my party arrived for dinner. We were greeted by a friendly host, which left us with a positive first impression (so crucial to any customer-facing business). Unfortunately, what unfolded next was so disappointing.

The restaurant was only half full, but we sat there for 10 minutes waiting for a server to come by, say "Hello" and take our order. I even caught the eye of two servers who each looked away and continued about their business. When a customer walks into your business, they need to be valued, respected, acknowledged and held in high regard. Whether your business is a restaurant or not is irrelevant. That initial meeting may be the one and only chance you get to make a significant impression. None of us are in a position to be lax and borderline rude to our customers and potential clients. I mention my lacklustre experience as a reminder that it's important to reflect on our own businesses, so we don't make the same avoidable mistakes. The truth is, I felt ignored and unwelcome, and I wasn't prepared to spend my hard-earned money in a place that had no sense of courtesy or customer service. We never want to make our customers feel that way.

The reason we're in business or have a job in the first place is because of our customers. They need to be at the forefront of our values and focus. It is inexcusable to make a client feel alienated.

How to keep your customer front and centre

- Observe and listen to your customers' wants and needs
- Remember your business isn't about you; It's about them
- Keep communicating (If the servers had said they were busy and would be over in a few minutes, I would have waited)
- Pay attention to details
- Don't take your customers for granted; Tell them you appreciate them
- Become customer service obsessed, constantly going the extra mile and being creative in the ways you communicate your gratitude and appreciation

- Make your customer a priority
- Apologise when you get things wrong; Own your mistakes, and put it right
- Don't just put it right, but leave them with a positive experience (Just like Microsoft did with a free 12-month XBox Live subscription)

CHAPTER 7

EGGS

"It may be hard for an egg to turn into a bird: It would be a jolly sight harder for a bird to learn to fly while remaining an egg. We are like eggs at present. And you cannot go on indefinitely being just an ordinary, decent egg. We must be hatched or go bad."
−C. S. Lewis

I actively have been looking at ways to improve my health and my waist line. I love my food, and I certainly won't be whisked up into the latest fad diet. I like sustainable lifestyle changes. I have had to educate myself in order to really undo some of my bad eating habits cultivated through the past 20 years.

I like to have eggs for breakfast, as I find they keep me full and my energy lasts longer throughout the morning. On this particular morning, I was discussing with my daughter how a chicken either produces an egg that won't hatch or one that will hatch into a baby chicken. The difference, for those who don't know, is in the egg. In order for it to produce a baby chicken, a rooster needs to mate with the chicken. Otherwise, the chicken will continue to lay infertile eggs.

The term "better together" has been sounding between my business ears these past few months. I can produce an egg on my own, but together we really can produce something alive and breathing. More than ever, I have been collaborating and joining forces with other likeminded individuals to leverage our combined influence and skill-sets.

One lady I met during my time in Austin left me feeling super fired up. Of all the meetings I had with various entrepreneurs and thought-leaders, she was the one who left me feeling inspired and challenged. With all due respect to all the incredible people I met in Austin, it was this lady who got inside my head and left me feeling super excited and buzzing with ideas. On the back of our meeting, we have collaborated on a number of small projects and are plotting our next venture together.

It wasn't just what this lady said, it was the way she lived and articulated a clear message to me that left me fired up. One mantra by which she lived was doing something dramatic with her life every seven years to keep growing and reinventing herself. She'd just uprooted her family from Denmark to move to Austin. In Denmark, she was someone many knew and respected. She decided she didn't want the comfortable life, but instead wanted to test herself and explore. She moved her family and business and is on a journey of self-discovery to bring success to her newfound business in Austin.

We must keep moving forward. We must challenge ourselves and those around us. We do that by meditating and dwelling on the right things because our thoughts produce feelings, and the feelings result in actions. When we take responsibility for ourselves, we then engage others. When we make an impression, we build a rapport and can begin to collaborate and build something of substance together.

We need each other to build something larger than ourselves. As entrepreneurs, we love to do our own thing and the freedom to express ourselves. But, in doing so, we limit our own abilities and opportunities and remain an egg. When, on the other hand, we join forces, we can evolve, grow and bring movement to the next level of our lives and businesses. We hatch. We all need a rooster or to be a rooster to someone else. As we invest ourselves into other people's lives and vice versa, we breed life and opportunity together. Collaboration enables both parties to grow beyond a single company or individual's limitations.

Points to consider when collaborating:

- Do you share a common goal or purpose?
- Do they have a skill or attribute you admire and may be lacking?
- Do they have the right mindset and attitude that

represents your key values?

- Will they challenge you and encourage you to deliver beyond your current capabilities?
- Will joining forces offer your customers something more meaningful?
- What is their level of experience and position in the marketplace?

CHAPTER 8

WHO ARE YOU?
WHO, WHO, WHO?

*"Efforts and courage are not enough without
purpose and direction."*
– John F. Kennedy

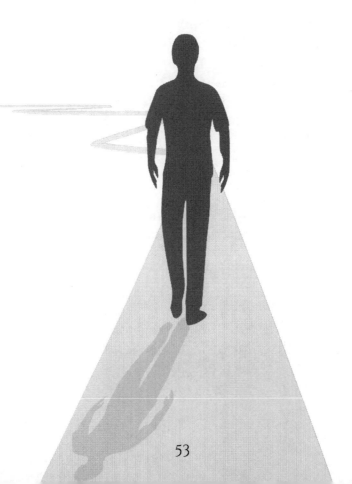

Knowing your purpose is the most exciting place to be. Sometimes, people die never knowing who they are or what they were put on Earth to do. People walk blindly hoping to find their true purpose. We all hope for an awakening that tells us who we are and what we're supposed to be doing with our lives. Sadly, it doesn't work like that. We have to pay attention to the gifts God has given us and then seek opportunities to be quiet and really get to know ourselves. It takes time to be still and reflective. It also takes courage to be honest with yourself and see both the good and those areas of your life that need polished and purified.

Getting to know the real you takes time, but it's worth it. Knowing who you are and what you were put on Earth to do are the most exciting and liberating times and revelations. Here are my seven tips to define your purpose:

1. **Focus on what you love.** What is it that you love to do? What excites you and gives you a buzz? What activities, situations or people create positive energy in your life. What innately draws you in, keeps you curious and keeps you moving forward? Is it a person, an opportunity, a product or service?

2. **Share your skills.** What makes you feel fulfiled? On what do people compliment you? At what are you naturally good? What skills, attributes or characteristics are recurring themes when people give you feedback or encouragement? Start asking those closest to you for feedback on your strengths and skills, asking what they admire and like about you. It helps to try an array of different tasks to see if you're naturally gifted toward a certain area.

3. **Identify who and what inspires you.** To whom or what are you naturally drawn? We are attracted to the people, places and things we want to be like or that resonate with us.

4. **Identify who and what you don't like.** When we look at the things that turn us off, upset us or frustrate us, it often can lead to our purpose by identifying the path we shouldn't take.

5. **Listen to what replays in your head like a broken record.** Think about the things you can't let go. What keeps you curious and asking questions? What have you tried to get out of your system but keeps popping up?

6. **Track your joy.** Simply write down a number from one to 10 with 10 being extremely high levels of joy and one being severely low. Write a few notes as to why you've scored the joy level as you have. If you scored a four out of 10, write down why. Was it a person? A situation? A circumstance? Do this exercise for a week, tracking the reasons why your days have either high levels or low levels of joy. This helps you start to increase or decrease the association of those things that have either a positive or negative affect on your happiness. Your purpose always will drive you forward and, fundamentally, take you to a place of inner peace resulting in high levels of joy and positivity.

7. **Contemplate what things people always come to you about.** What problem do people normally look to you to solve? Is it because you are well-connected? Are you a great problem solver? I have countless people come to me when they need an electrician or a plumber or someone to sort out their WiFi or a place to stay. People know me as a connector— someone who has a large network and likes to help pass business

from one person to another. Do you have something similar? Do you find people repeatedly come to you with the same wants and needs? Do they identify you for certain help or connections based on your attributes and skills?

Once you've defined your purpose in life, pursue it with all the vigour and intentionality you can muster. It really is one of the most exciting and liberating places to find yourself when you start contributing to life and community. It does wonders for your own self worth and sense of contribution to this world.

If you do nothing else with this book, make sure you find out who you are and then go spend the rest of your life living it out. When we live out of our authentic self, it liberates others to do the same and impacts the world like never before.

Here's a tool to help you find your purpose:

This is the Success equation from the Napoleon Hill Foundation:

P + T + A + A + F = SUCCESS

First, list 10 passions you have (P). These can be things you love or even things you hate. For example, you could really hate the child abuse that takes place in our world.

1.

2.

3.

4.

5.

6.

7.

8.

9.

10.

Next, list 10 talents you have (T). These are your skills and strengths. An example of this would be a talent to make someone laugh.

1.

2.

3.

4.

5.

6.

7.

8.

9.

10.

Then, list a mix of 10 associations (from businesses to people) with whom you would like to work (A). Make this realistic. Saying the U.S. President or U.K. Prime Minister may be a little too ambitious at this stage.

1.

2.

3.

4.

5.

6.

7.

8.

9.

10.

Next, compile a list of 10 actions (A) you need to take to do what you love (passion) with what you are good at (talent) with the people with whom you want to do it (association). An action may be to research your ideal customers or clients. Learning those details and communicating them effectively will have a massive impact.

1.

2.

3.

4.

5.

6.

7.

8.

9.

10.

Finally, create a personal mission statement. This is about how you want to be remembered (F). Understand the faith you have in yourself and your mandate to fulfil your purpose on Earth. Until you believe in yourself, nobody else will.

MY MISSION STATEMENT:

My mission statement is to have the influence to liberate, educate, support and invest in people and beliefs for which I have a strong conviction. I want people to feel I have given them something and never taken from them, whether through encouragement, wisdom, information, confidence, support or an ability to challenge them to be all they can be.

Once you know your why and what drives you, it helps you make better decisions. A job on an oil rig wouldn't suit me because of how isolated it is. I flourish by being around people, which then helps me make better decisions with regard to the opportunities and environments to which I say "Yes" and those I let pass me by. Knowing your mission helps you understand on what playing field you should be.

CHAPTER 9

CHANGING LANES

"Your power to choose your direction of your life allows you to reinvent yourself, to change your future and to powerfully influence the rest of creation."
– Steven Covey

If you drive, you'll know the concept of mirror, signal and manoeuvre is the correct etiquette to keeping you (and those around you) safe. Being conscious of what is around us (the mirror), navigating through life and being accountable to what and whom we are (the signal) and moving into the right position to find our identity and purpose (the manoeuvre) helps us assess situations, transition through life and create healthy boundaries.

In the car, and in life, the first step is to check the mirror. The great thing about looking in the mirror is you can see all around you to assess situations, risks and opportunities. This exercise gives you a chance to reflect on and make calculated decisions about what is ahead. You can see what is going on around you and in you, so it's a great opportunity to really evaluate your future state. Sometimes, we look in the mirror and forget who we really are. But, when we're honest, this snapshot allows us to make sound decisions.

The second step is to signal. This helps us transition from where we are now to where we want to go and gives us the necessary accountability to tell others of our plans. Most people, on reflection, do not fundamentally want to stay where they are within society or the world. All of us are moving forward and journeying to a better way of living— a life that impacts, gives back, produces fruit and contributes to the lives of others.

Having accountability keeps us on the right path. When we tell people where we're going, they can check on our progress. When we want to write that book or lose those 10 pounds, the more people we tell, the more accountability we create in our lives and the less excuses we can make. We can't afford to isolate ourselves because we were created to build relationships (remember the egg? We're better together). Accountability isn't about checking up on you like you are a naughty, misbehaving teenager. When done properly by people who have your best interests at heart, accountability is a positive attribute to your life.

When you signal your intentions, it helps both you and others by creating healthy boundaries that protect everyone. When people know you're responsible and empathetic, they're more likely to help you move forward on your own journey while giving you the necessary space to grow. We must balance our passion for moving forward with respect and wisdom to take us to where we want to go without inducing road rage in others by being so hellbent on getting our own way all the time.

The third step is to manoeuvre. This is the most important action. If we want to move beyond our self-limiting beliefs or the limitations others seek to put on us, we have to keep moving forward. We have to take action. We must position ourselves in the right mindset to continue on to success. The Roman philosopher Seneca said, "Luck is what happens when preparation meets opportunity." We must be prepared to put ourselves in the right position to seize the opportunities that lay before us.

This is a process. We must continually reflect and check our mirrors, paying attention to where we are and what we're experiencing. We must pay attention to the culture and environment in which we find ourselves. We must then signal, letting people know where we're heading, while being responsible for our own personal development. Finally, we must manoeuvre into new relationships, opportunities and adventures by taking up the right positions that play to our strengths, fan the flame of our passions and take us to where we want to go. When we are constantly moving forward, we limit the risks and chaos that could arise from being inattentive, unintentional and unclear in our communication and actions.

CHAPTER 10

FORCES OF NATURE

"Your energy introduces you before you speak."
– Unknown

In 2015, my favourite quote was, "If it's important to you, you find a way. If not, you find an excuse." My favourite quote this year is, "Your energy introduces you even before you speak." It hit me right between the eyes. I love its deep and profound meaning. When I first read it, it was one of those introspective moments, and it consistently has made me ponder and chew on such a revelation ever since.

The thing I really love about this quote is that it articulates a concept I struggle to express to others. I often am telling people to bring their A game or that their positivity, perspective and viewpoint is of critical importance.

I look around at all the people, opportunities and projects on which I have been working the past two years, and all of them were stimulated by and attracted to my energy. When you focus on your personal growth, the persona you convey is very much an introduction to who you really are.

Body language is powerful and fuelled by the way you see yourself. Walk tall with a desire to motivate, inspire and make a difference rather than intimidate and show off.

When we walk tall, we make an impression without uttering a word. People can feel your energy, enthusiasm and spirit. It's not only infectious but a super challenge and an exciting opportunity.

People make a decision about whether they like us within the first two minutes of our first meeting. If we're full of life (or what I like to call "juice"), we will make a positive impact before words even are exchanged.

We need to become conscious of our presence and what we're allowing to manifest before those with whom we seek to build relationships. We need to be wide awake, alert, responsive and reactive each and every moment of the day. When we're conscious of and enlightened by our own energy and what we are putting out in the world, we see a positive impact on ourselves and those around us.

Words can be powerful or they can be cheap when uttered without conviction. If we consciously focus on the nonverbal impression we make through our state of mind and body language, we can make an interesting and invaluable impact.

As we become better stewards of our minds and energy, we'll need no introduction. Instead, our spirit will introduce us and make the first impression. All we need to do is show up consciously and with purpose.

CHAPTER 11

MASTER YOUR ENERGY

"Managing your energy is more important than boosting your energy."
– Michael Hyatt

Are you a workaholic trying to find a way to keep your energy up and also find time to relax? Are you tired of struggling to keep it all together, while trying to squeeze in enough time to truly enjoy life?

Being the best requires us to take a close look at how we manage our energy because it is necessary for everything we do.

Entrepreneurs at startup businesses are working longer hours than ever before. You rise early and work late into the night. It consumes your mind and drains your energy. Time is finite. The number of hours in a day is fixed, but your energy is renewable. If you don't manage your energy, your relationships will suffer, your work performance will suffer and your general love for life will suffer.

As I said in *Inside Job*, even Formula One has pit stops to refuel and check the safety and performance levels of the vehicle.

Just like a race car, people need pit stops because scheduling breaks is essential to staying at your peak performance. If you don't manage your energy you will be unable to function to your maximum potential. It's like racing around with a flat tyre.

Let's take a closer look at the four energy wasters you should kick to the curb to tap into your primary sources of energy and stop busyness while remaining productive. Just because you're moving forward does not mean you're getting ahead.

Four energy wasters to kick to the curb:

Caring what other people think

It is important not to measure yourself by the standards of other people. This preoccupation with trying to please others quickly can lead to depression. The opinion of strangers should not matter. Wanting to please and take care of others is natural, but when pleasing others is based on the fear of rejection it can become habitual and unhealthy. You can combat this destructive habit by appreciating your inner loveliness. Whatever thoughts or feelings arise within you, respond to them with kindness. Life is not about pleasing others, it's about fulfilling your potential.

Worrying about the competition

Drive your business forward by following your purpose. Your competition isn't against other people but against your own ability and potential. Avoid people who are constantly bringing you down, and surround yourself with people who are positive and create an environment that helps you grow, be inspired and have the courage to tap into your own creative genius. Who you allow to speak into your life will affect the way you think and, subsequently, your behaviour and success. Rid yourself of people that criticise and speak ill of you. Pay no attention to these dream killers.

Wasting emotional energy on old, unresolved pain

We judge our pain and believe we are not entitled to it because the event occurred such a long time ago. It's important to acknowledge past pains and open the wounds so healing can begin and clear emotional space for lighter, happier feelings. You might need counselling or just a heart-to-heart with a trusted friend. Make an appointment, and let the healing begin.

Doubting and second-guessing yourself

Take a look at the root cause of your dissatisfaction, and address why you invalidate your own choices. Learn to trust yourself to make good decisions. Don't let the fear of making a mistake stop you from gaining new experiences. Keep a "proof" journal to record all the instances from your past where you have made good choices that have brought you happiness. This is your irrefutable evidence that you have the ability to make forward-propelling decisions.

CHAPTER 12

ENERGY MATTERS

"I do believe we're all connected. I do believe in positive energy. I do believe in the power of prayer. I do believe in putting good out into the world. And I believe in taking care of each other."
– Harvey Fierstein

When we manage our energy, we boost our motivation, performance, creativity and memory. Your energy can be broken down into four different elements:

Physical Energy

We all know inadequate nutrition, exercise and sleep diminish basic energy levels. We will have trouble managing emotions and focusing attention when our physical energy is depleted. Physical energy is the fundamental source of fuel in our life. It's imperative we eat right, get enough rest and exercise regularly. We hear all the time from the nutritional experts to keep our glucose levels sustainable by eating regularly.

Fitness: Exercise increases the supply of oxygen to our blood stream at any given time. Going to the gym creates a "cornerstone habit," which is a habit we can build other habits around. After we have a consistent fitness habit, we're ready to tackle any other challenge more easily. Exercise also releases endorphins, which are energy and mood boosters.

Sleep: Go to sleep and wake up at the same time consistently. Research at Loughborough Sleep Centre shows your performance will become inconsistent with even the slightest sleep deprivation. Not getting enough sleep disturbs your cognitive function. Quite simply, it makes you temporarily stupid. Get enough rest. Tiredness and sleep deprivation results in poor decision making. You will not only protect but absolutely increase the reputation of your brand by coming from a place of rest, recovery and focus.

Emotional Energy

When you're able to control your emotions, you can improve the quality of your energy regardless of the external pressures you may be facing. Emotional energy has a specific feel. It is a sense of grounding and trust. One that finds the calm at the centre of a storm. It's a sense of peace amongst the chaos. It's a sense of being happy, forward-looking, resilient, hopeful and creative. High emotional energy means you can ride out any storm, take on any challenge and maintain courage through it all.

Mental Energy

Mental energy is your ability to concentrate, analyse and be creative. It's essential to directing your focus on the activities most important to you.

Your mental energy can be zapped by excessive worry and negative thinking, leading to an inability to concentrate and focus. Underutilising mental energy by watching an excessive amount of television or sticking to rigid routines can result in a don't care attitude and demotivation. Your frame of mind will determine how effectively (or ineffectively) you allocate your physical store of energy. A commitment to learning new things every day is one of the best ways to keep your mental energy sharp.

Focus strategically on activities that have the most long-term leverage. I have come to understand unless people intentionally schedule time for more challenging work, they tend not to complete it or will rush through it at the last minute.

Spiritual Energy

You need to align your values and goals with a purpose beyond your immediate self-interest. You must immerse yourself completely in your mission. What I mean by that is you must be present in all you do. This doesn't mean sacrificing the quality time you should prioritise with your children or loved ones, but it does mean giving the best of yourself to every endeavour, whether that is starting a business, managing a career or caring for your family. Find the why in your life, and you find your purpose.

Be aware of what you want because indecision is the enemy. Empower yourself to make the right choices to showcase your passion and skills. Create and protect time to think and invest in you. You must stay centred on your mission statement. I make sure everyone I work with produces a mission statement for their life. Mine is, "To have the influence to liberate, educate, support and invest in people and beliefs in which I hold a strong conviction. To put my money where my mouth is and to leave my mark on all people especially my children, family and friends." Take time to consider what you want your life to represent and for what you want to be remembered when you leave this Earth. Getting clear on your personal mission will help you focus on the right things and prevent you from drifting far away into unhealthy or destructive territories. Understanding your key reasons for being here will only serve you and keep you on the right track.

When we are on the right track, we will come to appreciate the words of Dr. Phil McGraw, "Life is a marathon, not a sprint." Don't be busy. Be productive. Even a fool can be busy.

Everybody wants a piece of our time, but be wise to whom you choose to give it. Explore curiosities, but be intentional. Do everything with purpose. I have noticed that the brain attempts to simulate productive work by avoiding big projects and focusing instead on small, mindless tasks to fill time. Don't allow your time to be choked up with busyness, and don't accept tasks just because someone will pay you for it. Only accept tasks that are in line with your passions and strengths. Be mindful.

Take time to reflect. Reflection is one of the most important tools for personal growth. It's helpful to take time out to take stock of how you're performing, what you're doing and what's taking your energy. Discover what motivates you, and make it your personal mission statement.

Stop multitasking. It dilutes your focus and execution. When you're doing more than one thing at a given time, you're not giving 100 percent of your energy to anything. Focus on the most important thing in the moment to save energy in the long run. Focus on one thing at a time. Find that one thing, and become an expert. Rid yourself of duties that no longer stimulate your passions or give you the opportunity to flex your skills. Ensure technology serves you. Don't be a slave to the distractions of social media. As someone who spends a decent amount of time on social media, I manage and analyse the results of my efforts. Seventy percent of my business comes through the powers of Twitter and LinkedIn. Those kinds of results ensure my level of engagement online is worth my time. However, if social media is used in a way that makes you spend hours merely browsing or looking up the next new gadget or plotting your next vacation, it's not going to serve you the way it should. When it comes to social media, I rarely automate my Tweets or messages because I believe you need to be present and engage in the moment rather than a day or week later. Have a clear, dedicated amount of time you want to spend on social media daily and then lay some ground rules. The power of social media is in the engagement with clients and potential customers. When you are on a social platform, be present and don't do it in between something else. Take time to listen and focus on your audience. In the words of writer Publilius Syrus, "To do two things at once is to do neither."

Know what matters to you, and focus on that. The only way to make your life extraordinary is to know what extraordinary means to you. Once you know what matters, set your priorities accordingly.

Some ways to set priorities:

Schedule down time. Take regular time to switch off. Carve out regular breaks or take time to reflect, unwind and enjoy the fruits of your labour. Often, when we take timeouts, we tap into our creative genius.

Build strong relationships. They are key for social health, and they do your heart good. Embrace the spirit of community by building a network and culture that supports, uplifts and blesses those around you.

Establish a great reputation. Your reputation is the best and most valued commodity you have as a business owner. You won't function well on empty fumes, and you'll harm your reputation when you push yourself beyond what's healthy.

Express gratitude and appreciation to others. Holding gratitude in your heart does amazing things. Most profoundly, it multiplies. Nurturing a grateful heart demonstrates appreciation for what is good in your life right now.

As entrepreneurs, we often feel overwhelmed by the need to go all in, never slowing down or exhibiting weakness. Yes, it's up to you to keep the momentum going, be 100 percent focused and motivate your team, but you should never feel guilty about breaks. One of the reasons I schedule my energy and allow myself downtime is to avoid burning out. This way, when I commit to a client, I have enough energy to fully mentor and motivate them to become their best selves. Manage your energy by getting enough rest and exercise and by avoiding energy–depleting people. Focus your attention on things for which you have a passion and that align with your purpose.

Energy Action

Each night, before you go to bed, identify the most important challenge for the next day, and make it your first priority when you wake.

PARENTHOOD

"There is no greater name for a leader than mother or father. There is no leadership more important than parenthood."
– Sheri L. Dew

Just as I consistently work to master my energy, so too I constantly challenge myself in the way I raise my children. It wouldn't sit right with me to be the greatest mentor I can while sacrificing being the greatest and most present father. What would it say about me to impact relative strangers to the detriment of investing in the little people I helped bring into the world?

I love being a dad more than anything and love each of my children in their own unique and special way. Any man can be a father, but not every man can be a dad. I pride myself on investing in these incredible little human beings. Each of them have their own character, skills and areas to grow and develop— we all do.

I keep myself accountable to the impact and investment I place within each of them. I regularly carve out one-on-one time to be present for them. We all know children spell love "T-I-M-E." I'm intentional about seeing each of them grow and develop and be able to stand on their own two feet. Our children are home schooled by mummy. The premise of home schooling is really to help kids become lovers of learning while educating them in the essential areas of math, English, reading and writing. You then focus in on the subject matter toward which they naturally gravitate or in which they show an interest. According to an empirical analysis published in 2010 by *Widener Law Review*, called Evidence for Homeschooling: Constitutional Analysis in Light of Social Science Research, "Homeschooled children achieve levels of academic achievement similar to or higher than their publicly schooled peers. These results cut across racial and socio-economic lines."

Numerous studies demonstrate that homeschooled students obtain exceptionally high scores on standardised academic achievement tests. For instance, one nationwide study analysed data from 1,952 homeschooled students across the country and found the "students, on average, scored at the 80th percentile or higher in every test category (i.e., reading, listening, language, math, science, social studies, study skills, etc.). The national mean for these standardised tests, by contrast, was the 50th percentile." Sharpening a child's passions and interests helps them develop an early sense of exploration and realise the importance of investing in the areas where they have an innate desire and inclination. This process really draws out the entrepreneurial spirit in each of them.

We know, as adults, the key to a fulfiled life is one spent doing what we love and earning a fair wage out of it. If, at a young age, our children are able to follow their instincts and own who they are, this dramatically will impact the choices they make growing up and strengthen their relationship with themselves through trusting their gut and making time for what they love.

The Bible says we're to raise our children in the way they should go and they will not depart from The Word. What this scripture means is that we should raise and train our children within the context of this proverb and what the Bible already tells us ("that all Scripture is God-breathed and is useful for teaching, rebuking, correcting and training..." (2 Timothy 3:16). When we educate our children in the truths of Scripture, it helps them become wise (2 Timothy 3:15); gives them the tools and knowledge to do good acts (2 Timothy 3:17) and prepares them to be mindful of cultures. We have a huge responsibility as parents to steward, guide and mentor these little people. I cannot neglect my children and their development for anything. It's true you can give a man a fish and he will eat for a day but teach a man to fish and he'll eat for a lifetime. Everything I've learned from my experiences, mistakes and successes must be passed on to my children. We can't live our failings and disappointments through our children. Instead, we must support them to flourish and grow in what they love.

Lois is the eldest child, and she has become fanatical about football. She has been playing since she was 5 years old and really has developed over the past three years. I'm so proud of her. She inherently is a little shy, but when she runs onto the field she comes alive. Lois is fearless on that pitch. It always puts a smile on my face to see her tackle, run and dribble— especially since the majority of the kids she plays against are boys. At times, she gets knocked to the ground and a part of me wants to run over, pick her up and comfort her. I hold back because I know that would be the wrong thing to do. She needs to find her own way. Lois never moans when she's hurt. She dusts herself off and gets up again. A boy knocked her to the ground recently. It was a total accident, and she didn't allow the situation to upset her. Instead, she picked herself up and carried on playing. Her attitude pleases me. It's very easy (and we are all guilty of it) to play the victim, but accidents do happen. I guess that is life. We can allow past wrongs to stay with us for years and years or release them from our lives. Lois didn't take the incident personally. She accepted it was part of the game and didn't let a negative experience stop her from doing what she loves. If mummy and I are encouraging Lois and showing her how to behave, it leaves me no doubt she'll go far. You can't control someone's attitude or viewpoint. It's a personal choice. However, you can set the example and hold people accountable for their attitude and the consequences it may bring with them.

Casey, our son, has been doing Taekwando and is beginning to see bursts of testosterone course through his body. We needed to find him something to help him express himself and siphon off some of his pent-up energy and frustration. Martial arts suits him and his personality. He also is learning some key disciplines and finding something he can call his own. I'm not yet sure if he has a passion for it like Lois does with football, but it's important we encourage him (but not force him to do things he may not love doing). I think curiosity is keeping him interested right now. When you see your child doing well at something, it's very difficult to know what to do when they falter between quitting and continuing on what seems an almost daily basis.

We must give children enough responsibility to do something with their life and figure things out for themselves but not too much that they feel overwhelmed and don't get to enjoy the journey of their childhood. The challenge for me (and all parents) is in how we are raising our children. What values and beliefs are we instilling in them? Are we encouraging them to follow their heart and become lovers of learning? Are we putting our work first ahead of our responsibilities to raise our children to be the best they can be? We mustn't lose track of the impact we are making in our children's lives.

CHAPTER 14

LESSONS FROM CHILDREN

"Children are our most valuable resource."
– Herbert Hoover

As humans, we can learn from just about anyone if we're able to humble ourselves, watch and observe. Being the father of three incredible children is a huge privilege and also what I believe is my greatest work. I love to watch them play and interact with others. I love the questions they ask, full of mystery and curiosity. As they grow older, their character starts to develop and results in the most beautiful personalities being born.

When my youngest, Eva, turned 2, she began to talk. It was the most adorable and moving transformation I'd witnessed. She has a beautiful spirit and an energetic and witty personality. There were three words she started to say often, and each word captured my attention and got me thinking. It was these three words that started to speak to me and created a clear pathway for me to learn something.

Here are three things I learned from a 2-year-old:

EAT

What are you feeding your brain? Who's nourishing your mind? Where are you going to be fed? Eva constantly was asking to eat. It got me thinking about not just what we feed our bodies but about what we are feeding our brains. What we put into our body impacts the strength and substance of our personality, character and influence.

I started to ponder Eva's hunger. She was hungry to eat so she could grow and develop, but hunger is a missed opportunity when we fill our bodies with the wrong food. Likewise, the wrong stories, beliefs, people and thoughts negatively affect our mood, influence and ability to create the opportunities we need to move forward.

UP

Eva has a limited view of what she can see and experience. She is not able to see all that's in front of her. When we first start out in a new job or launch a new business, we are relatively small. We are unknown and have limits in relation to our position in the market and our credibility within our industry. We need time to grow.

Eva was saying, "Up," because she wanted a change of view. She wanted to see what I was seeing. She needed and wanted a fresh perspective. She felt limited. Perhaps, Eva felt like she was missing out and wanted to experience a new world.

In life, we all can get bogged down by the responsibilities of adult life. By soaring to new heights, we're able to get a fresh perspective. When we hang out with people who are larger than ourselves with regards to wisdom and knowledge, we're able to shift our perspective and take a step up to the way they see things. This, in turn, results in a shift to the way we operate and perceive things.

NO

Not enough of us say, "No." We feel a sense of guilt when we do. We say "Yes" out of obligation and don't fully understand what we are committing to, which can result in us feeling over-burdened and stressed. We need to create boundaries. I use three filters when contemplating commitments. If the opportunity doesn't fulfil my filters, I say, "No."

My Three filters:
1. Does this excite me?
2. Does this play to my strengths?
3. Does this give me the opportunity to move forward?

Be empowered to say, "No." Eva already knows her own mind. Eva will need to learn to consider others, but I love that she knows what she wants. Of course, it always is about balance. The moment you know your own value, someone will call you selfish because you're no longer accepting just any old thing that comes your way. The flip side is you're creating a life you own and giving your energy to the people and projects that excite you. This always creates the biggest impacts on your life and on others. I would much rather hang with people who know their value and purpose in life— there's little that's more appealing.

Make sure to integrate the words "eat," "up" and "no" into your lifestyle. From what and whom are you eating? Around whom do you need to hang to be lifted up and get a fresh perspective? To what and whom should you be saying, "No," to protect your happiness and nurture yourself and those you most care about.

When we continually make errors in judgment by agreeing to people or projects out of guilt and people pleasing we will wind up miserable and frustrated. I encourage you to get in the habit of saying, "No," so you can protect and nurture the people and projects to which you should be saying, "Yes."

When you can't see the forest through the trees, it's imperative you find a different perspective and outlook. Try seeking counsel from those who have gone before you to gain some much needed wisdom, recommendations and strategy.

Be heedful what you are feeding your mind. Our thoughts produce feelings, and those feelings produce actions. Get the mind firing on all cylinders and soon you'll be in your zone and acting in tandem with your values and spirit.

CHAPTER 15

HAVE CONFIDENCE IN SAYING, "NO"

"It's only by saying "No" that you can concentrate on the things that are most important to you."
– Steve Jobs

We live in a world filled with people pleasers. This is true of all the nice people I know. They find it hard to say, "No," because they love to care for people. There is nothing wrong with caring for people until you are frustrating and exhausting yourself. If you are one of these people, you may need to start creating boundaries to protect your sanity and happiness.

When we commit to everyone and everything, we burn out and are no good to anyone. Saying "No" is healthy. We mustn't keep saying "Yes" only to wonder why we're so stressed and tired. I've already mentioned three filters I use before making any decision. If an opportunity doesn't excite me, play to my strengths or help take me where I want to go, I simply say "No" to it. This prevents me making mistakes and let's people know what I may or may not entertain.

There are some parallels between our relationship with fire and our inability to say, "No." It's no secret people struggle to say "No" which results in pain, frustration and difficulty. Often, people cant say "No," because they're riddled with guilt and feel a sense of obligation. Of course, there are times we need to do things we don't want to do. This isn't about that. What it is about is the overall culture of how we govern and lead our lives. If you're constantly saying "Yes" without considering the implications, it will inevitably lead to problems.

If I put my hand into a flame, it will burn and cause me pain. As we grow older and understand fire burns, we learn to respect what fire can do to us and restrain ourselves from touching it. By respecting fire, we develop a relationship that enables us to work with it in a way that serves us rather than harms us. We can use fire to keep us warm, cook food, burn rubbish and light a candle. When we are respectful of fire, it will protect us, but if we overstep the boundaries it could again result in being burned.

Our inability to say "No" is exactly like putting our hand in the fire. It inevitably will result in pain. That's where the term "burn out" comes from. The fire will consume you, taking all your time and energy until there's nothing left. When we learn to say "No" it serves us, protects us, keeps us warm and gives us the energy we need to invest in worthwhile people and opportunities.

Personal boundaries are really to protect you. We all need them to ensure correct etiquette is upheld in how others treat us. When you establish personal boundaries, you are underpinning your own self worth. When your boundaries are violated by others, you can respond how you deem appropriate. You can establish your own boundaries based on your past relationships and life experiences. Boundaries help you establish your own preferences within relationships.

It's important to reflect on your relationships and on the things to which you're saying "Yes" when you should be saying "No." Take responsibility for the decisions you make. When you start saying "No" to someone to whom you've always said "Yes" there may be some fall out or some confusion. Take time to think about what you'll say to that person. A good way to approach a potentially difficult situation of this kind is to ask the individual if they'd like you to be polite or honest. In most cases, people choose honesty. In this way, you're able to share that you need to introduce boundaries to protect and nourish yourself rather than saying "Yes" out of guilt or obligation. In doing so, you'll take back control of your life and all the demands that go with it. It won't be easy and will take time to cultivate, but remember when you continue to say "Yes" instead of "No" you're putting your hand in the fire.

CHAPTER 16

CHANGE THAT DIAPER

"Changing a diaper is a lot like getting a present from your grandmother— you're not sure what you've got but you're pretty sure you're not going to like it."
– Jeff Foxworthy

Just as too many people are afraid to say "No," way too many people are sitting in their own mess. Stop being so negative, dwelling in self pity and being so down on yourself. This world is tough enough without the constant self harm we inflict each and every day through the conversations we have with ourselves. It's not healthy to stay focused on the bad things in our lives, so stop wasting time feeding your brain with unproductive clap trap.

It's time to change that diaper. We can't keep carrying our pain, mistakes and shames around like a smelly mess. Ever wondered why people don't get close to you? Why they keep their distance? It's because you stink. You need to flush away the past.

When we carry our mess around, it weighs us down. It's not just a question of smelling bad, we also walk funny. Sometimes, we need help to deal with our mess regardless of how embarrassing it is. Sometimes, getting real with others serves us better than going it alone.

Take care each day to cleanse your mind and focus. Babies are bathed before being put into freshly laundered clothes for bed time. End the day the right way by focusing on gratitude, cleansing and feeding your mind with positivity. Be aware of what's going on in your mind and endeavour not to go to bed angry, depressed or anxious. End each day right by finding a way to cleanse yourself. I do this through prayer and gratitude, taking time to reflect, be one with myself and settle any internal disputes or upset.

We want to be fun to be around. We are all on a journey of self improvement and need to get in the habit of dealing with our own mess behind closed doors rather than exposing others to it. The issues of life do not need to be paraded around before an audience. We don't go to the bathroom with the door open. Maybe you do if you're in a relationship, but you get my drift. We need to deal with our crap behind closed doors. That may, at times, mean we need to bring confidants into our private setting to deal and work through the rubbish in our lives, but we don't venture out into the world with all our mess and stench on display.

The key here, really, is to address the issues privately with a trusted mentor, friend or accountability partner. That way, we can look at the issues without burying them. Receiving help and counsel from others will only increase your chance of success and personal growth. It is a very humbling thing to allow someone to wipe your backside or, at the very least, allow a trusted friend to tell you your attitude stinks. We all need a positive nucleus of friends who will tell us what we need to hear instead of what we want to hear.

Stop focusing on the bad and get out of your smelly diaper. It's costing you friendships and opportunities, but it's also definitely holding you back. The problem with sitting in your mess is it starts to irritate you, make you itch and makes it difficult to find peace in your own skin. If we want to grow, we must be intentional about dealing with the issues that have the biggest impact on those around us through the way we think, act and behave. We can ill afford to parade around our negative views, open wounds, fears and insecurities and expect to be welcomed and received into other peoples' environments. Instead, choose positivity.

How to get out of your own mess:

- Acknowledge the aspects of your life or thinking that need changing
- Practice self care and reflection to understand your present state

- Become self aware (if you don't know you stink, you will do nothing about it)
- Listen to the feedback of those you trust, and see if you need to take action and make changes
- Take a shower. In other words, take a break to mediate or pray about current issues or thoughts you are carrying that may need work
- Ask for help— we all need it from time to time

CHAPTER 17

CHANGE OF SCENERY

"To get away from one's working environment is, in a sense, to get away from one's self; and this is often the chief advantage of travel and change."
–Charles Horton Cooley

It's a sunny morning. The day is filled with hope and expectation, but by 9 a.m., my first few meetings have been cancelled due to unforeseen circumstances and I'm left with an open three-hour window. It's been raining for days, yet today has greeted me with sunshine. I'm often a little disappointed when plans get changed because I believe in commitment followthrough. So, I am feeling a little blue and decide to drive out to the country to enjoy this sudden free time and go on a date with myself.

As I drive to a secluded area, I feel the stress and disappointment of another cancelled meeting leave my body as my mind begins to drift to what is ahead. We will never get back today, so we had better make it count. I shout out, "Plot Twist," and soak up the spontaneity of the morning ahead.

I walk through the gardens and then through the trees. My boots are wet from the morning dew, as I try to avoid falling down the badger and fox dens surrounding me. I take some deep breaths. I feel the sun on my face. I can feel a oneness arising in me. Being a city boy, I always get excited being out in the country where I can stretch my legs and be one with my thoughts. Out here, I can listen to nature without the distraction of traffic and the normal bustle of people.

A change in environment is all I needed to shift my mood and release the disappointment and frustration. Sometimes, we have to leave our normal environment and explore. Human beings are not meant to be confined. We are called to roam, explore and see what is all around us.

This vast open space is liberating, and I feel 100 times better than when I first looked at my phone to find meetings were cancelled. We have to take responsibility for how we feel. Get out of the familiar. Go explore. Change our environment. We all face struggles and have a barrage of emotions flood our hearts and minds daily. Yet, this little action of taking myself away, leaving behind the normal and exploring the unfamiliar has greeted me with positivity. I'm feeling invigorated with a sense of clarity and purpose.

What is your environment like? When was the last time you ventured out and explored? We can't always take a vacation, but a morning out of our busy schedules to explore and go on an adventure can really have a positive impact. My adventure encouraged me to continually listen to my intuition rather than wallow in disappointment. Instead, I've taken a positive action and helped myself. We learn from the environment in which we live. The outdoors are full of life, new beginnings and nature. It sparks our creative flair. The colours, smells and organic growth of nature gives our minds and spirits the environment we need to burst forth with new ideas and imaginings.

Often, as busy professionals, we don't have the luxury or ability to take whole weeks off on vacation. Sometimes, short little day trips do the trick. One such day trip stands out from amongst the rest.

I went to the Galleries of Justice in Nottingham a few years ago. It was a great historical experience. We all were given a crime number (a crime number is given to each offender to record their personal information and their alleged crime with details to track vital information when standing before a judge and jury) and had to face a judge and jury as in the olden times. I was accused of rape and theft and sentenced to imprisonment and the capital punishment of having my hands removed. I was thrown into this dingy, dark and volatile environment for 20 minutes. I actually started to panic a little even though it was a reenactment and only a short time. This perfectly articulates the power of our environment. Sometimes, we need to have the courage to leave the familiar. We need to be wise with the places we end up settling, dwelling, living and even visiting because they always have an effect— either for our good or for our harm.

A positive environment for me is often when I go for my bimonthly massage. I have a great client with a successful massage business. Thankfully, she makes time to issue therapy to me. Here, the environment is a key ingredient to create the atmosphere and ambiance that arouses the mind, body and spirit to a place of peace and rest. Unlike the prison, this room is beautiful with lots of natural light flowing through the window and the smell of burning candles and body oil permeating the room. The freshness and comfort of the sheets and the sound of a waterfall sets the scene for tranquility. This is a place I can rest, be still and let the cares of my mind leave my body. I am no longer surrounded by noise, demands, responsibilities and distractions. I can be one with myself— quiet, still and comfortable. Massage is powerful.

Every person, entrepreneur or not, must take the time to change the environment in which they live to get a different perspective. Life can be hard and cruel at times, so it's important to consider where we're spending our time and attention and whether that atmosphere is serving us and conducive to our sanity and personal development. When we're constantly giving of ourselves, hustling and trying to get ahead, we need to take care of our body and minds. I get a massage to shift my mind and mood and relieve stress and tension.

Whether it's a regular massage, quick day trips or longer vacations, finding stillness in a busy world is key to your personal happiness and professional development.

CHAPTER 18

WALK YOUR FEARS

"I learned that courage was not the absence of fear, but the triumph over it. The brave man is not he who does not feel afraid, but he who conquers that fear."
– Nelson Mandela

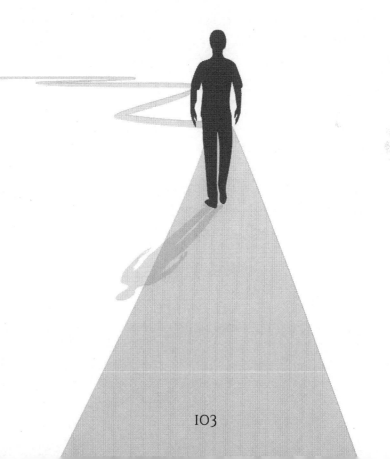

Fear can be debilitating but, when harnessed and channelled appropriately, it also can be a great motivator. One of the key strategies to becoming a more successful person is dealing with fear in a positive and constructive manner.

Everyone experiences fear. I know I do. For most of my life I was terrified of dogs, fearing they'd tear me apart. Did you know dogs actually are able to smell fear? This, of course, made me even more afraid. Seventeen years ago I made a decision to face my fear head on. So, I started walking a friend's dog. It was a terribly uncomfortable experience at first, but after walking the dog a few times the fear no longer had a hold on me. I took away its power and rendered it helpless.

We often allow fear to hold us back from reaching our fullest potential, but you can use that fear to change your life and shape your future.

What is fear?

Fear is a natural part of life that we often face throughout our journey. It arises in situations of perceived threat or danger. It has been placed within each of us to prevent us from doing foolish things like jumping off a roof. However, fear also emerges during stressful events, such as exams, public speaking, a new job or even going on a first date. We face mundane fears every day (like fearing we don't fit or fearing our cars aren't flashy enough). We also are faced with huge fears on a global level, such as acts of terrorism. These give us all reason to be concerned and aware of danger but, just like Nelson Mandela said, regardless of the fear (whether it be big or small, justified or crazy), we must choose to do it anyway rather than stay stuck in fear. This is true bravery.

Fear is a powerful emotion and has a strong effect on our mind and body. It is crazy to see what happens when we experience fear. First, our senses pick up the signals from our surroundings and send them to our brain's threat centre. This area, called the amygdala, sounds the alarm. The flight or fight response kicks in. Our heart beats faster, our breathing speeds up and our body prepares for battle.

There are two types of fear:

1. **Conscious Fear.** When we see something and interpret it as fearful. We do still have an element of control with conscious fear. We can choose to interpret these situations in a more constructive and positive way.

2. **Primary Fear**. This is our automatic response to something dangerous (like a lion chasing you). We don't need to question this type of fear, as it protects us and serves to ensure we trust our intuition and back away carefully.

Philanthropist and author W. Clement Stone said, "I think there is something more important than believing. Action! The world is full of dreamers, there aren't enough who would move ahead and begin to take correct steps to actualise their visions." I couldn't agree more, and I believe the primary cause of this is fear.

It is interesting to hear about all the different fears with which people battle. Your most terrifying fear may be a walk in the park for me, and vice versa. I love speaking on stage in front of thousands and, yet, I fear never having an audience. You, on the other hand, may love quiet and being in the background, while the thought of being front and centre scares you to death. When I look at the fears common to every man, this is what I see:

- **Extinction.** Fear of ageing and death. This is that panicky feeling you get when peering off the roof of your house. Funnily enough, I have found I am like a fine wine and get better with age. I accept the fact that we all will die. So rather than be afraid of it, I try and live my life doing what I love and focusing on personal and professional progression. It's greatly helped.
- **Mutilation.** The fear of losing any part of your body. My fear of being mauled by a dog would fall into this category.
- **Separation.** Fear of losing a job or loved one. This fear encapsulates rejection and abandonment. Coming from a broken family, this is a fear I have had to overcome. The fear of rejection was, and continues to be, a very real fear for me. Not measuring up and fearing someone telling me "No" is difficult but, through time and God's healing, I have found freedom and understanding. I've ultimately learned I can't control someone else's behaviour and actions; However, I can control mine. If someone rejects me now, rather than getting upset, I simply realise I am better off without them. Remember, relationships in all forms need to be of mutual benefit and value.
- **Loss of autonomy.** The fear of being trapped, immobile or paralysed. This fear is more commonly known as claustrophobia, but it also extends to our social interactions and relationships. The greatest thing about being entrepreneurial and creating your own business and income is that you are in control of your time and on what you spend your energy. The thought of being under someone else's employ again feels like a set of handcuffs to me.
- **Ego-death.** The fear of humiliation and shame. Did you know, three out of four individuals fear public speaking? As I mentioned earlier, I love public speaking and get quite a buzz from it because I love to share stories and the privilege of people taking time to

listen to me. Yet, for others, the thought of speaking in public is terrifying.

While fear needs to be overcome and sometimes we need to power through the fear, there are occasions when feeling scared is a real and helpful feeling. It can protect and preserve us. In most cases, however, we need to overcome it. Here are five ways to do that:

Five Ways to Overcome Fear

Change your perception

You can overcome most fears by changing the way you view them. Fear is like a construction worker vigorously waving his red flag back and forth, warning you to stay where you are. Do not come any closer. There's danger ahead. In reality, fear is trying to derail your progress and prevent you from reaching your next level of achievement. See the red flag of fear as a key to where you need to proceed. It's amazing that the times when we have moved forward and overcome our fear, we suddenly realise we magnified the fear beyond rationality. Most fears are irrational. They are possibilities but not certainties.

A dear friend of mine used to refuse to fly. She was petrified, so she wouldn't step foot on a plane. This resulted in her missing out on lots of adventures and business opportunities. Then, one day, she was invited to an incredible opportunity in New York City, and her friends convinced her it was worth looking this fear in the eye and overcoming it. Was she scared and nervous when she stepped on the plane? Of course she was. It took her a number of hours to begin to settle and a little alcohol to help her push through, but she did it. The trip to NYC was significant for her and opened lots of doors for her professionally. This would never have happened without the ability to push herself, challenge her limiting beliefs and take action. Now, don't get me wrong, she still doesn't love flying but will no longer allow her ongoing fear to decide her decisions or prevent her from taking action.

Build your courageous muscle

By lifting weights consistently, you're actually causing tiny tears in your muscle fibres, which the body then repairs. Your body adapts, grows and strengthens that muscle to better lift weights in the future. Just like weight training, you need to flex your courageous muscle consistently to help it grow stronger and more resilient to life's challenges. It may not be comfortable and it might even hurt, but you'll be better able to take on opportunities and challenges. Do things that test your limits.

Do it anyway

When you feel fear and it's holding you back, just do it. Take action. Show up when it would be easier to run away. This will give you a major boost of confidence and advance you toward greatness.

Leave your comfort zone

Try new things. Author Brian Tracy said, "Move out of your comfort zone. You can only grow if you are willing to feel awkward and uncomfortable when you try something new." Heed his advice and venture into the unknown. If nothing else, leaving your comfort zone will be very exciting.

Pray

God will give you the strength to deal with fear. He has put talents and gifts in you that you will be able to discover only when you face your fears and push past barriers. He will guide you to breaking free from fear. Never let fear stop you from reaching your fullest potential. Be fearless,

Whenever fear shows up in your life, you now know it's an indicator that your breakthrough is near. Do not let the little fears common to man stop you from moving forward. You don't need to concern yourself with the car you drive or the house you live in. When you do what you love, you'll begin to find you're suddenly making the money you need to upgrade those little luxuries.

The larger global fears we face are harder to overcome because the accessibility to knowing all that's wrong in the world is now at our fingertips in our mobile phones. When the plague broke out in London, you never knew about it until you had it. Now, with the power of the Internet, if you are sick and look up your symptoms online it will say you have cancer and light the flame of fear inside of you. We must take responsibility for what we read and to what we listen. Much of the fear-mongering isn't helping you, but it is feeding your fears. Terrorism, on the other hand, is a huge concern and a legitimate threat to which we can't be blind. While we must be vigilant and aware, we also mustn't allow our fear of it to stop us from living and making the choices we deem correct for our lives.

We live in an age where fear is prevalent. Fear rears its head in so many different forms. Some fears are easier to identify than others. The fear of fitting in can feel very real, but it isn't life threatening. A fear of terrorism, on the other hand, has the whole world taking notice. As mentioned previously, we should not allow terrorism in any form to bully us and prevent us from taking the actions we believe are right for our lives. That said, it would be foolish to not carry out due diligence and be vigilant about those things that could put our lives in danger. Mandela was right when he said our challenge is to overcome fear and move forward without freezing in our tracks or allowing our fears to dictate our forward momentum.

Our world, and often our governments, are built to ensure we don't deviate too far from the path of safety. The normal path is one that starts with us attending school and perhaps going onto college before finding a job and working until we're 65. Most societies are built this way and want each of us to follow that path. This path began during the Industrial Revolution. Daniel Priestly, author of *Entrepreneur Revolution*, talks about a new movement— the entrepreneur revolution. To join that revolution, you must have courage in the face of fear. You have to believe your ideas can grow wings, fly and really bring something powerful or disruptive to the marketplace. Any person who ever achieved anything had courage to overcome obstacles and believed, despite adversity, setbacks and self-doubt, what they were on to was significant.

So, how do we build that courageous muscle I mentioned earlier? How often do we allow fear to rule our decisions? Any choice we make based on fear will not serve us. Instead, it puts us into places of compromise and uncertainty.

In the gym, we see people taking hold of weights and dumbbells to strengthen and build up muscle. They're habitual in completing their reps. As I've already said, when our muscles are torn down, they begin the process of being built back up— only stronger. Building your courageous muscle is the same. The stronger it becomes in overcoming fear, the more it can carry, hold, push, pull or move. I don't know about you, but I want to surpass my current achievement and skill. When we build our courageous muscle, we give ourselves a greater opportunity to advance beyond our current level of skill and understanding.

Our courageous muscle has to be put under pressure to flex and develop. The first way to build this muscle is by honing our tolerance for risk-taking. We must have the audacity, drive and balls to not only take risks but to enjoy doing so. This is a learned trait. Our greatest failure is not in making mistakes but in being too lazy or fearful to leave our comfort zone to try something new or build something that could fail. Our greatest learnings come from our ability to push ourselves, test the waters, be curious and even be willing to come across as a little silly or naive in our quest to achieve something of value and substance. When we take risks, we grow. When we grow, we step into some of the highest levels of joy. I know from both personal experience and working with my clients, we experience the greatest joy in life when we grow personally and professionally.

The next way to build our courageous muscle is to put our head above the parapet. In so doing, you are putting your head on the figurative chopping block instead of backing away from responsibilities. We need to always own our beliefs and attitudes so we can admit when we get things wrong. We need to identify our values and keep them front and centre to stay on track and be a leader in our respective industries. Every time we're willing to step out and show our authentic selves or are willing to take a hit because others don't agree, we become courageous. When we stick our head above the line, we must be prepared to get punched in the face. That's why it's vital we stick our head above the parapet only when it's in keeping with our key values. Being punched in the face is never going to be pleasant, but it's better to be punched in the face for a cause in which you believe than for anything else. We must stand up for our beliefs.

Facing our fears head on is the third way to strengthen our courageous muscle. I have a friend who is petrified of heights. She doesn't do anything by halves and, in keeping with her go for the gusto mentality, decided to book herself into a skydive in an attempt to face and settle this fear once and for all. I spoke to her about the experience and, unsurprisingly, she was petrified. She even had to tell the tandem instructor to physically push them out of the plane. The skydive began with tears streaming down her face and a lengthy, terrified scream. The experience really pushed her to the brink. But, as she began to settle and started to see the ground below in all its glory, she found enjoyment in it. That enjoyment opened her eyes to all the things fear previously had prevented her from doing (like attending sporting events and posh networking functions in tall buildings). Her fear had impeded her, but she looked it in the eyes and overcame it. Overcoming fear results in freedom, and freedom results in more choices. We can't limit our options in life based on fear of things that may or may not happen.

The fourth way to build your courageous muscle is to do the things others only talk about. While words are powerful, they also can be cheap. If we say something without really meaning it, it becomes an empty and futile vow leading nowhere. We need to take action. Each time you step up, take a risk or try something different, you build that muscle of courage.

The final way to build this muscle is to find others who face the same battles as you. I wouldn't normally recommend hanging out with people who carry the same burden as you because your environment is paramount to your growth and opportunity to overcome challenges. I would rarely advise an alcoholic to hang out with other alcoholics. However, I would recommend it wholeheartedly if both parties are serious about freeing themselves of addiction. When we journey side by side with people who are in the trenches with us and whose vision and desire is to get out of there, we can become each other's advocates. When we bring our courageous muscles together, we find the power of synergy and collaboration. The point is not to feed the fear but to work together and move forward using creative ways of challenging and helping each other.

Challenges to build your courageous muscle:

- Book something into your schedule over the next 30 days that makes you uncomfortable but you know will benefit you when you overcome it
- Write a blog or produce a vlog for the next two weeks about the ways you are becoming more courageous
- Let others know about your plans to overcome a fear, so they can hold you accountable
- Talk about your fears to a few trusted friends, and ask them to help and encourage you
- Create your own strategy to tackling a fear. If you have a fear of public speaking, start by doing a short video where you record yourself delivering a small message. While the environment may be different, the confidence you have to articulate your thoughts and feelings into words is half the battle when talking to large crowds

CHAPTER 19

CONFIDENCE

"Inaction breeds doubt and fear. Action breeds confidence and courage. If you want to conquer fear, do not sit home and think about it. Go out and get busy."
–Dale Carnegie

I already have alluded to the fact that we must continually invest in our own confidence. In the dictionary, confidence is summed up as "the feeling or belief that one can have faith in or rely on someone or something."

Think about at what you are really good. What natural ability have you been given? Perhaps, write it down and just ponder the strength of that skill. Own it and acknowledge that it's been placed there to serve this world. While it's always great to have confidence in someone or something outside ourselves, the best way to start building confidence is from within. We build confidence by repetition and by planning ahead of time. In some ways, there is crossover with building your courageous muscle. Courage is being brave without knowing the outcome— there also is a degree of uncertainty in confidence.

People who know me say I'm confident, and I am for the most part. But, I'm equally human and open to vulnerability. It's taken time for me to build self-confidence and sometimes that becomes a hindrance in my walk with God. I'm certainly guilty of being self-reliant, which doesn't always serve you well in the Christian faith. However, I know God is confident and knows what the outcome will be for me. We are a reflection of Him. I see confidence as building yourself up not from a place of pride but in a healthy belief that you matter and can contribute to this world when it counts. I want that for everyone and encourage you to stand up and grow bigger than your problems.

Sometimes people mistake confidence for arrogance, but there is a clear distinction. Arrogance elevates an individual above others, resulting in them feeling insecure and inferior. In arrogant promotion of yourself, you're in danger of degrading others. Confidence, on the other hand, is being sure of who you are and betting on yourself to deliver. Living this way inspires and challenges others to do the same. We can't be weak. We have to be strong yet teachable. An arrogant person won't listen or learn, while a confident person knows they have to keep growing and learning to manifest more confidence in life.

The first step to confidence is being prepared. When we perform due diligence and put in the training, hard work and focus to master our craft, we have every right to be confident in our ability to succeed in the opportunities before us. If you want to be confident, you have to be prepared. You need to know your stuff and constantly develop yourself. I already mentioned the Seneca quote about luck being preparation meeting opportunity, and even Oprah Winfrey's definition of luck is "when opportunity meets preparation." I love it! When we're prepared, we can seize every opportunity that comes along. It is pure laziness and foolery to expect things to just happen without any degree of planning and preparation. Opportunities will come your way this year and you had better be ready to take them.

So how do we grow in confidence?

Daily habits to build your confidence:

- Smile! It actually affects our internal energy and improves our body language
- Dress according to the image you want to convey and what feels most comfortable to you
- Look people in the eye, and give them a firm handshake. If you look and act confident, people will have more confidence in you too
- Practice speaking to yourself, being assertive but not aggressive. This will help you deliver a better and more influential message
- Create your own affirmations, and meditate on them
- Plan your day the night before. When we plan what

we want to achieve, we gain control of our day rather than our day controlling us

We all like to engage in conversations and love to share what's going on in our lives. For the most part, that's perfectly fine and healthy. Be mindful, however, that when we focus our conversations on problems, they impact not only your confidence but also the confidence others have in you. We must appreciate problems from a positive point of view. Our self talk and the conversations we have with others can have both a positive and negative effect depending on the focus you place on the situation. Always look for the opportunity in each problem you face.

Turning our mistakes into lessons is a surefire way to grow confidence and take responsibility for our actions. We're all human, and we get things wrong. Some mistakes are more costly than others, but we can find reassurance that nobody is perfect. Remember, whenever someone points a finger at you, there are always three fingers pointing right back at them. When we reflect, admit our mistakes and apologise if necessary, we grow in wisdom and learn valuable lessons we should embrace and for which we should be grateful.

I was called out on a quote on my web site that appeared as my own. When I researched it, I was embarrassed to see it was part of a song lyric from a very well known artist. I subsequently changed it and made Wiki and Google my new best friends. It was an innocent mistake, but it upset people. I'm humble enough to acknowledge my mistakes when I get things wrong.

We all make mistakes. When you put yourself out there, experiencing new things and entering new territories, it is inevitable. We have to take the learnings, put our hands up when we get it wrong and take the lesson. This will significantly impact your confidence level and make you more relatable— while you're good at what you do, you're also human.

Lastly, convey a real appreciation when someone does right by you, says something kind, compliments you or buys you a gift. When you exude the appreciation of someone who is truly grateful for an act of kindness, it impacts you to the core and lifts your self confidence. When you realise you matter to others and are truly appreciative of this, it causes a positive ripple across your relationships.

CHAPTER 20

UNBROKEN

"If you can take it, you can make it."
– from the film Unbroken

If you have read my first book, *Inside Job*, you will know I love my films and to quote or explain something meaningful I've gleaned from their stories. It is a powerful way to articulate a point so people can relate.

I watched *Unbroken* with a friend at the back end of 2014. It was a book first and was made into a movie by Angelina Jolie. I always have enjoyed movies based on true stories, and this one was no different. The film is based on the experiences of a prisoner of war during World War II. It is a heroic tale about overcoming obstacles and challenges that would take most of us to the brink.

The film is all about the life of a U.S. Olympian and soldier, Louis "Louie" Zamperini, who spent 47 days at sea on a life raft after his plane crashed into the water during the war. The raft was spotted by the Japanese army, and Louie was taken to a POW camp.

Like all great movies, the film seamlessly melds an expansive time frame, weaving present and past into an incredible story. *Unbroken* covers some of Louie's childhood struggles, such as breaking the law and the cops chasing him and his partying lifestyle. One day, Louie was caught looking up a woman's skirt and his older brother, Peter, witnessed how quickly Louie could run as he fled the scene.

Peter encouraged Louie to use his amazing speed to better himself, so he began training as a runner. Incredibly, Louie went on to represent the United States in the Olympics. While he finished in only eighth place, Louie did break a world record for completing a lap in the quickest time—faster than any other man in history.

The film then returns to the life raft where Louie and his fellow officers are lost at sea. Sadly, after a number of days at sea, one of his regiment passes away. Through it all, the group is faced with many challenges, including sharks circling the life raft and being shot at by a Japanese war plane, which damaged the raft. But, Louie perseveres, making a pact with God that if he made it home to his friends and family, he would live the rest of his life for God. Finally, the group is found by the Japanese and sent to different camps.

Like all POW camps, leaders at the camp where Louie ends up often flogged and beat prisoners for information. But, Louie was not giving any away— even when beaten severely by the camp's man in charge, Mutsushiro Watanabe aka "The Bird."

The Bird knew Louie was an Olympian and often tried to break his spirit, singling him out and pushing him to the edge. One of the punishments Louie faced was when his fellow soldiers were forced to punch him as hard as they could or risk being shot and killed. In this harrowing and brutal situation, Louie encourages his countrymen to hit him to avoid paying the ultimate price. Even seeming kindnesses were designed to bring Louie to the edge. For example, he was able to appear before the Japanese media to let family and friends know he was alive. After that, The Bird dangled the carrot of additional privileges if only he would turn his back on his country by participating in propaganda efforts. Of course, Louie refused and ended up back at the POW camp.

After several years and countless beatings, The Bird was promoted and left the POW camp. Unfortunately for Louie, things came full circle after American forces bombed the first camp and Louie ended up back under the control of his adversary at a new camp.

True to form, The Bird exposed prisoners to gruelling conditions. On one particularly hot day, Louie became exhausted while lugging coal. He took a quick respite and was dutifully punished for his rest. The Bird made Louie lift a huge piece of wood above his head with the warning that he would be shot if he dropped it or even lowered his hands at all. Incredibly, Louie remains unbroken and defiant. The Bird, finally realising he would be unable to break Louie's spirit, falls to his own knees. He can't understand how a man could possibly keep going under such extreme conditions.

When the war is finished, Louie returns home, hugging and kissing the ground. Louie fulfiled his promise to God from the life raft and went onto become a Christian evangelist. He even later went back to Japan to meet The Bird to issue forgiveness but was stood up by his tormentor.

Here are 10 things I learned about life (and business) from *Unbroken*:

1. **Change your environment to channel who you are.** Louie constantly was getting into trouble with the law and the police. He got caught up in the wrong crowd due to the environment to which he exposed himself. He spent half his childhood running from trouble and trying to escape law enforcement officers on the back of his regular stealing habits. It wasn't until he discovered his love of running (encouraged by his older brother) that his life started to shift in a different direction. We can all have the right skill but, without the right platform to express it, it often causes more harm than good.

2. **If you can take it, you can make.** There is a lovely scene where Louie is training. He is running down a country lane with his older brother encouraging him while riding his bike. It's clear the run is arduous and stressful by the strain on his face. We all go through periods of discomfort, tension and pain. We must

match it with focus, discipline and grit to power through rather than lose hope or quit on the road. We need someone to come alongside us and give us hope and a willingness to never surrender. We need to surround ourselves with people who hold us accountable and believe we can achieve greatness. Peter says to Louie, "If you can take it, you can make it." This mean, if you don't stop, if you push forward, you can make it. You can do anything if only you don't quit. It's powerful! A positive voice and an encouraging word can be the difference between failing and making it.

3. **Have a daily and habitual training regime.** We all need to be consistent and habitual to achieve respect and trust. Louie was no different. He put in the hours of training and dedicated his lifestyle choices to reflect those of not only an athlete but an Olympian. Success, I am convinced, is doing the foundational elements many people don't want to do. When we do the mundane and boring foundational work of hard graft, sacrifice and persistency, we are more likely to be successful.

4. **Be resourceful.** When Louie was at sea in the life raft, the crew became extremely hungry. We all need to look around us and see the resources and people at our disposal. During times of extreme hunger, Louie focused on the hundreds of albatrosses around their raft. One came and sat on the top of the raft, and Louie grabbed it with his hands and killed it. The same was true of sharks who circled the raft. Louie took what was hunting him and turned things on their head by killing the shark for food instead. We must constantly survey what and who is around us. What will serve us, keep us alive and help us grow versus what will hinder us, attack us and pull us down.

5. **Hold onto hope, and create a vision.** There's a famous proverb that says, "Hope deferred makes the heart sick." We all need something to hold onto— something to believe in. Even if there is only a glimmer of hope, it can do wonders for our hearts and minds. Too often, we allow our circumstances to be a death sentence that results in a permanent outcome. When the truth is that our circumstances are only temporary. The hope for a better tomorrow is possible. Louie constantly looked to encourage the others in the life raft. We have to look beyond our circumstances, beyond the current state of affairs and believe things will change.

6. **Be courageous.** I already have dedicated a chapter to courage. It makes perfect sense that courage was at the very centre of who Louie was and how he overcame such incredible odds and brutality. When Louie wrestled sharks, he was willing to risk his life and sustain severe injuries in order to feed himself and his crew. Over and over, you see Louie brimming with courage and never shirking responsibility. He never buckled. He put his body and mind on the line time and again. Each of us must survey the risks and decide it is, in fact, more risky to stay in the comfort of the raft and die of hunger than to wrestle the sharks.

7. **You can't conquer what you won't confront.** Louie had so many encounters with The Bird. He was tortured, abused, beaten and brutally attacked on so many levels. It is quite overwhelming that he didn't break, but endured and faced his bully. Louie stood in the face of adversity, and didn't shirk from the incredibly painful attacks. Louie overcame his adversary through sheer resolve and grit. We can conquer nothing in this life without first confronting it. Often, we have to look at our situation or obstacle right in the eye and plant our feet rather than run

from pain, hurt or accusations. The only way we will ever overcome anything is through our ability to confront it and stand our ground.

8. **Do what's right, and not what's easy.** After meeting with Japanese media and conducting a radio interview on the back of his capture, Louie was offered the opportunity to live a life of luxury in a community run by the Japanese government. He would no longer be a POW if he turned his back on America. Louie did no such thing. In life, we always are presented with options, but too often make the mistake of taking the one that feels good and looks appealing on the surface. We live in a society that encourages us to follow our emotions and do what feels good. With wisdom and experience, we learn that just because something feels good doesn't mean it's always the best course of action. We all need to live an honest life, to walk openly with high levels of integrity. Taking the right road is often the hardest road. How tempted must Louie have been? Hungry, tired, beaten, frustrated, mentally and physically challenged and handed a carrot of opportunity to go from prison to palace. Yet, he decides to stay in hell knowing his soul's freedom is more important than his physical freedom. Louie's decision challenges me to the core. I must strive to do what's right over what's easy. That often looks like things I don't want to do.

9. **Take one for the team.** That awful scene where his own countrymen are lined up one by one to punch him in the face is brutal. Two hundred men collectively punching him over and over again because failing to do so resulted in death reminds me that sometimes we must take one for the team. We have to make sacrifices for family and friends. We have to be willing to carry deep responsibility. We have to protect them by taking the hit ourselves. We must lead, guide and

protect those we love even if it leaves us picking up the pieces.

10. **Issue grace and forgiveness.** It's incredible after the ordeal and how much he was wronged and beaten Louie still wanted to find forgiveness and extend grace and mercy to those who had done him wrong. He actually went back to find The Bird after some years, but he was unwilling to meet. Still, Louie was ready to forgive him and release the pain and hurt rather than carry it in his heart. Forgiveness always is more for our benefit than for the benefit of the one who wronged us. When we hold onto the wrongs and hurts others have caused us, we prolong the agony and can't move beyond the pain in our hearts.

CHAPTER 21

GRATITUDE

"Gratitude unlocks the fullness of life. It turns what we have into enough, and more. It turns denial into acceptance, chaos to order, confusion to clarity. It can turn a meal into a feast, a house into a home, a stranger into a friend. Gratitude makes sense of our past, brings peace for today and creates a vision for tomorrow."
–Melody Beattie

A grateful heart and mind always result in blessings and growth. It's remarkable how the times I focus on what I have rather than on what I don't always result in an abundance mindset. We all want more. We all want to see improvement. There always are things with which we're unhappy or things we want to see differently in our hearts and lives. The issue with focusing on problems is that we can become overwhelmed, depressed and bitter. There always will be someone better off than you— and others worse off too. We waste time and energy focused on things with which we're not pleased. The magic happens when we focus on what we have and on those things that bring us happiness (like our child's development or playing a particular sport).

There are five ways I bring gratitude into my life, and I want to share them with you in the hope you'll benefit, grow and unlock the gratitude within you. Interestingly, when I'm more grateful, I actually find further blessings and breakthroughs in my life, which only results in more gratitude. It's a wonderful cycle. The more grateful you are, the more good comes into your life. Try it for yourself.

1. **Keep a gratitude diary.** It builds up that abundance mindset. Regardless of how bad your day has been, there's always something for which to be grateful. Some gratitude may be simple, like a sunny day, while others may be specific, like picking up a new client or contract. As I mentioned in my previous book, *Inside Job*, I've been keeping a daily gratitude journal for three years, and it's done wonders for my ability to be grateful for what I have in my life and appreciative of those around me and the opportunities I've had to impact others.

2. **Handwritten notes.** Another great way to increase gratitude was adopted from a client who sent a weekly handwritten thank you card to two people in her life. It showed these people she cared. Proverbs 11:25 says, "He who refreshes others will be refreshed." When we do good by someone else, it has a positive impact on our own thoughts and emotions. Taking time to reach out to those in your network and say "thank you" will only ever strengthen your bond with that person, which ultimately is good for business and building your reputation as a person of integrity.

3. **Speak your gratitude into the universe.** Expressing my gratitude to God is something I endeavour to practice regularly. I'm grateful for the gifts, skills, opportunities and people in my life. When I thank God for what he's given me, I put myself in a place of trust and reverence before him. Whether you believe in God or the universe or some other spiritual source, being grateful for the things in your life cultivated by something larger than yourself is an important part of the process.

4. **Reflect on your relationships.** Being grateful for your relationships with others is a powerful way to increase gratitude. Try reflecting on what your parents have done for you. Think about the importance of your friendships. Be grateful to your mentor or coach for their wisdom, reassurance and challenges. I'm super grateful for two men in my life with whom I meet regularly to journey through what life and business brings us all. We take time to hang out, chat, share issues or frustrations and soften the blows life sometimes throws. I'm so grateful for who they are to me. They take time out of their own busy family lives just to have some quality time. We don't get to choose our family, but we do choose our friends. When someone makes time for you, appreciate and value

them, and be sure to let them know it. It's important we create a relationship culture. Among other things, that may mean creating a small group for yourself of likeminded people to focus only on building each other up and overcoming obstacles. One-to-one friendships and larger relationship groups are powerful.

5. **Focus on you.** Finally, stop comparing yourself to other people. Your race isn't against the person to your left or right. It's against yourself. Create an environment and build a culture that taps into your creative genius. That may mean simply creating your own daily affirmations you believe to be true about yourself. Positive affirmations create an environment that is both self-fulfilling and very liberating. I spend very little time focused on my competitors because I want to sharpen who I am rather than defer to the way others are doing things. There are thousands of coaches and mentors out in the world. Why do people work with me? Because they like me, trust me or know me. We need to be vulnerable enough for people to see who we really are and professional enough for people to trust us with their deepest stories. It is a privilege to work with people and encourage them to really discover who they are without any fluff or having them simply pop a few positivity pills. When we embrace and invest in our own style, it sets a precedent of trust that becomes appealing to those around us. I want to do business with people I like and trust, as do we all. When I bought my latest car, it was important to me to buy from someone I liked as much as I liked the car. I found several similar cars and the same make of car from several dealers and, yet, I didn't overly trust any of them. The man from whom I did finally buy was someone who knew who he was and celebrated his own personal style.

One of the great things about writing books is getting feedback from readers. I have received many emails from people all over the world thanking me for writing *Inside Job*. One common theme (through the different habits, ideas and strategies) is that the daily practice of gratitude has made a big difference in all their lives. A number of readers on the back of *Inside Job* shared little testimonies of what they now do to impact gratitude:

Michael Hatton, Owner of Zeus IT, said, "After reading/ listening to *Inside Job*, I looked at gratitude in a completely different way. I realised there were so many things in my daily life that I was grateful for. Whether I wrote them down or just took a few minutes each day to reflect on my gratitude, it made me appreciate the things I once took for granted. Those little experiences and feelings, that happen most days, when considered from a point of gratitude really do fill you with a sense of prestige and privilege."

Ann Marie Anderson, Group HR and recruitment, also shared what she's implemented after reading *Inside Job*. "Sometimes, saying "Thank you" is all it takes to show your gratitude to someone. Sometimes, it takes more. How do we know what is best? How do we make a decision on this? How do we ensure that we do, or say, something to show our gratitude? We're all individuals and have our own way of demonstrating gratitude. One thing is for certain— everyone must do or say something. We all have something to be grateful for!

In my own life, gratitude is embedded into my day as much as breathing, eating and sleeping. If I'm sleeping, I have survived another day, dealing with personal challenges, laughing and even crying. Most of all, at the end of the day, I am grateful to be alive.

My life is as complicated as I make it, and I like to make it uncomplicated! I value and am grateful for my family, friends, neighbours, work colleagues, my adorable Golden Retriever and even strangers with whom I come into contact. I like to smile and find that most people will smile back— even strangers! To some, this smiling addiction is contagious and therapeutic. Would you agree? Smile now, and look at yourself in the mirror or even your mobile phone for a smiley selfie (#smileyselfie). That's better, isn't it! Now, go and smile at everyone you see. If we all do this, we can spread the wonders of smiling and improve our health and wellbeing.

Think about this— The person or animal you smiled at just now may be the only smile they receive in their day, so you can make their day and demonstrate your gratitude simply for being alive. It really is that simple.

Now, spend a little time at the end of your day before you go to sleep and write down other things for which you're grateful.

To summarise, I back myself and the strengths and skills I bring to the table. I focus on what I am good at on what brings me joy. Add to this my gratitude to the amazing people in my life and the way my God has nurtured me, and it all helps when cultivating gratitude. The simple habit of keep a gratitude journal and sending out thank you cards to those who have blessed and touched my life is a simple way to keep blessings and opportunities flowing. The more grateful you are, the more goodness that will flood your life. The more goodness in your life, the more gratitude. That's the kind of cycle we can all get behind."

Rebecca Marsh, Owner of English Rose Cake Company, said, "Gratitude is a simple notion. It is easy to be grateful but harder to practically apply to daily life. Why, for that matter, should one need to? I personally never used to think about the power of gratitude. Of course, I was grateful for lots of things in my life, but I never made a habit out of reminding myself what those things were. After reading the chapter on Positive Habits in *Inside Job*, it became clear that unfortunate things can happen every day (things that make us feel low, uninspired, doubt ourselves, etc.) but getting into the daily habit of naming what I'm grateful for shrinks those negative experiences and thoughts through the power of more positive ones.

The way I use gratitude now is, in the morning, I keep a daily journal of to-do lists, future tasks, thoughts, etc., and adding gratitude to it was simple. I found writing even incredibly general things down like, "I'm happy for my health," or "I'm grateful for my education," helped programme my thoughts for the day in more a positive light. No matter what happened to me that day, I always had something to be grateful for. The effect that's had on me in other areas of my life is incredible. The positive reinforcement means I handle daily tasks differently. I may notice an opportunity I wouldn't have seen or been open to if I had allowed negativity to consume me. People around me bounce off my positive attitude, and this all has a ripple effect to creating a positive, happy life. Don't get me wrong, some times are harder than others, but as long as you reinforce that positive habit of gratitude, the rewards keep on giving."

CHAPTER 22

THE POWER OF REFLECTION

"The real man smiles in trouble, gathers strength from distress and grows brave by reflection."
– Thomas Paine

Around the end of December, I always reflect on what I've achieved during the year. I love looking back on my accomplishments. Reflection provides a sense of purpose and adds meaning to your life. During these last days of each year, I'm not only looking at what I accomplished, but at what I didn't quite pull off and even at some mistakes and failings. Reflecting on mistakes and failings is not a negative exercise. When failure is addressed in a constructive way, it can actually be a powerful aid. This activity rarely brings up negative emotions. Instead, it helps me identify areas for growth and maturity. There is opportunity in failing.

An important component to reflection is the development of key takeaways to use as guidelines moving forward. Annual reflection often reveals powerful insights and personal revelations that begin to form part of your value system.

Last year, I had three distinct revelations that now serve and help me on my journey, as I navigate through life and its challenges. I'm confident my personal revelations also will speak to you.

1. **Actions over intentions.** I must judge myself by my actions and not just my intentions. I find most of my mistakes come in how I act upon good intentions. I always mean well. I'm not wired to cause harm to others. I want to see people flourish and grow and really live a fulfiled life. Yet, 95 percent of my mistakes last year were based on me having the right intention but the wrong execution. One of the takeaways is really understanding that everybody isn't like me. I need to carefully consider my audience and with whom I am communicating. What works for me may not work for

someone else. I need to continue to think and explore the options before I take action.

The only way to grow is to hold our actions to the same high standard as our intentions. Our behaviour is a reflection of our internal belief system. If we believe something is okay, we behave like it's okay. For example, if a person believes they have no personal value because of a poor opinion of themselves, then they'll act irresponsibly and exhibit a depressed victim attitude.

Beliefs manifest as behaviours. A person may start hanging around with the wrong crowd and making poor choices to validate low self worth. In order to change behaviour, we first must change belief. Once you're fully aware of your own value, you'll start to act differently and may begin evaluating your friendship groups. In extreme circumstances, you may realise the people with whom you once hung around are actually no good for you. We must take responsibility for our actions even if they have been misunderstood.

2. **Self worth and self esteem.** When we have a healthy opinion of our own value, we stop putting ourselves in vulnerable positions with people who either don't care or don't know how to tender kindness to our hearts.

   I love being encouraged. One of my love languages is spoken through words of affirmation. People really can build me up by what they say to me— it gives wind to my sails. However, this has to be coupled with my own beliefs. Encouragement never can replace the value you put on yourself. A great question to ask yourself is, "Do I like myself?" That may be a difficult or uncomfortable question, but the answer will enlighten you about how you see yourself.

As with anything, we have to find balance. Shoot for a healthy opinion of yourself rather than an inflated one, which only leads to arrogance. We have to take responsibility for our ability to know our own value and back ourselves to succeed. Your internal dialogue is a key indicator of whether you back yourself in most situations or self sabotage. While I appreciate other's belief in me, it's only when coupled with my belief in myself that there is opportunity for an impact in my life. The best way to make a difference in other people's lives is always to make a difference in your own first.

Actions to sky rocket your belief in yourself:

- Write down 100 things you have accomplished so far in life
- Meditate on all the things you have overcome to increase confidence
- Recall times you found a solution to a problem
- Continually invest in yourself
- Surround yourself with people who believe in you
- Go on dates with yourself, and enjoy me time

3. **Likability.** Not everyone is going to like me, and that's okay. As human beings, we have two common emotional needs: To be liked and to be loved. It's inevitable, when you wear your heart on your sleeve like I do, that the words people say can be sown deep in your heart. If we don't uproot them, they can grow and take up residence there. If you give me the choice, of course I want to be liked. When people say hurtful or untrue things, it can spin you down a road of depression and self pity, but when we have a healthy value of ourselves, we can admit our problems, apologise if necessary, take the learnings and move on without beating ourselves up.

The great thing about people not liking you is you know very quickly where to focus your attention. When we know not everyone is going to like us (or sign on to be our client or customer), it can be very liberating. We don't need to be liked by everyone. The people who are supposed to run with you will. Those who fall to the wayside or try to stick the boot in often are jealous or misunderstand your intentions and actions. Sometimes, people feel threatened when you're making inroads, and they're scratching their heads wondering why they're miserable and not moving forward in life.

Once I realised I didn't need to be liked by everyone, it helped me relax. We are never going to please everyone. The more you trust yourself to have standards and create boundaries, the more you'll stir up people who want to knock you off course. This is when having a trusted and tight network helps soften the blows. We need a strong circle (a community of loyal friends) who will surround us and encourage us during difficult times of criticism, challenge and uncertainty. That's why I talk about the power of investing in meaningful relationships throughout this whole book (and in life generally).

CHAPTER 23

HOW TO GIVE BIRTH

"One sure way to bring in the new is to make room for it."
—*Akosua Dardaine Edwards*

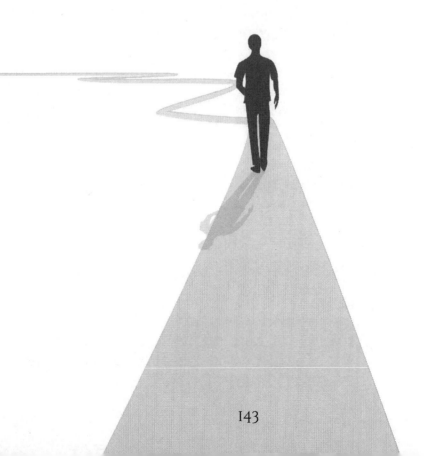

We all go through various forms of pain and tension that often can feel like the whole world is against us. We have to go through difficulty and challenges as we grow and journey through life. Allow the pressure and constrictions of life to fully manifest, so you can birth what's within you.

I love to daydream and allow my imagination to run wild for a moment. Have you ever sat down on your favourite chair or on your favourite mountain and just given yourself permission to imagine and envisage a world of possibilities? When you have a dream about which you're very passionate, you think on it, maybe writing it out and creating a dream board or other visual aid to stimulate and encourage you on your path toward achieving it. When we have a dream, we often dwell on it until it consumes our thoughts. As we consider the possibilities, we think about how it would feel to be living out our dream. We all love to daydream and paint pictures that aren't yet our reality but hope soon will be.

I always think carrying a dream is very much like a woman carrying a baby. The idea first is conceived. It then needs time, food and energy to help it expand, develop and mature. Nobody can see what is working behind the scenes, but within each of us are the core seeds that, when nurtured and cared for, develop into a healthy, amazing reality. It will take time. You may become uncomfortable as the dream starts to manifest itself into reality. People may say you're different because something is changing inside of you. They may say you're carrying yourself differently. It is inevitable that life changes, and people notice when we are carrying the heartbeat of a new idea or concept within us. This often begins with very small and subtle shifts in priorities and time. We all were created to dream and have vision for our lives. So when the dream is conceived, we start to feed and water it. We invest time, energy and care into really focusing on the intricate details of life.

It's one thing to dream, but it's another for that dream to grow within us. The moment your dream becomes bigger than you, it's time for it to be birthed into the world. I have witnessed the birth of my children, and each experience was different. I have no idea what it must feel like for a woman to go through such a mix of emotions, pains and joys in the space of a birth. I have seen firsthand the need to try and figure out how to give birth. From trying varying positions and deciding which (if any) drugs to take to ease the pain, to whom you want in the room when your baby is born, the process certainly is no picnic, and I can only admire females for their tenacity and courage in this respect. I am sure any woman who has given birth will vouch for how painful but worth it is the process to have a new life lying on your chest.

It amazes me that, despite the ordeal, women want to, and do, have more babies. The joy and exhilaration rank higher than the pain and discomfort a woman must go through not just at birth but through the whole process of being pregnant and, ultimately, a mother.

Remember, for those going through personal or professional discomfort in life, before birth there always is great pain.

How to give birth to your dreams

BREATHE

Meditate and be quiet to find peace in the midst of struggle. It's important to stay one with ourselves and focus on the task at hand. If we come from a place of assuredness, it will help us with the next phase of clarity and wisdom to work with the contractions instead of against them.

CONTRACTIONS

Don't resist the contractions. Work with them. We need contractions and discomfort to help birth what's within us. It's this very tension that brings the movement and change necessary to bring that product, service or relationship to the fore. Anything of value will always cost you something.

ACCEPT HELP

We all benefit from the expertise of those who have been there and done it. If we want to transition from dreams to reality, we must be humble enough to listen to the wisdom and counsel of those who have gone before. Those who have birthed ideas into the world have great knowledge to which we would be foolish not to pay attention.

PUSH

Don't work against God or the universe. When it's the right time to push, give it everything you've got. You will know when to push when the tension becomes too much and your dream becomes bigger than yourself. When your dream wants out, don't resist it. Instead, give it the platform it needs and deserves to make a grand entrance. Don't be surprised if your dream comes out crying. Like babies, startups, innovations and new concepts often need to cut their teeth. When this happens, it's time to show comfort and security by being responsible and allowing others to help you develop and improve the offering.

Don't be afraid of the pain and discomfort. Instead, be encouraged, invest in your dreams, give them life and let them grow until they're bigger than you. Prepare yourself for birth. Remember to breathe, and don't resist the contractions needed to bring out what's within you.

We only get one chance at this life. Some of us only get the honour of having one child and some of us have to fight to become parents at all. We all have the imagination and seeds of ideas, concepts and blueprints to bring something unique and impactful to this world. It will cost you something. There will be challenges and difficulty. When your dream, finally, is birthed, it will need feeding and care. No man or woman has ever been successful without sacrifice, hustle, grinding and busting your chops to bring into the world the dreams and visions you have in your belly. If you have a baby (vision or dream) growing inside you, nurture it, take care of it and feed it the right things. Don't put the wrong things into your system and cause a defect. Be responsible. If you have a dream, it was given to you for a reason. It is now your responsibility to make it happen.

CHAPTER 24

STARTUP FAILURE

"Many of life's failures are people who did not realise how close they were to success when they gave up."
– Thomas Edison

Why do entrepreneurs and startups fail? Your business is not about you. It's about your customer! I often am asked about the most common reasons entrepreneurs fail. The truth is, there is no one reason why entrepreneurs (or any of us for that matter) fail. It's a collection of reasons, choices and fundamentals. I think the first thing to say as a way of encouragement is to understand that if any of us wants to be successful in our lives and our businesses, we have to accept that success often means experiencing failure and taking the learnings, while dusting ourselves down and going again. I love Thomas Edison's mindset when he said, "I have found 100 ways of how not to make a lightbulb." Rather than focusing on the failings, he focused on the positive. We all need to do that more.

One of the fundamental reasons entrepreneurs and startups fail is because their product or service doesn't solve a problem. If you want to make a stupid amount of money, you have to find a solution that speaks to millions of people. The more people your product or service affects, the more scalable it is and the greater your chance to make an impact and have a healthy bottom line. There are too many businesses that offer the same product or service with varying degrees of quality but not enough to sway loyalty. If we're going to bring a product to market, it either needs to be completely original or significantly better than the status quo. Plenty of entrepreneurs make enough money to pay their bills and afford some luxuries, but if you really want to make an impact and have some wealth your product or service needs to solve a problem. A great question we should all ask ourselves is, "Why does my customer or client need me?" The answer forms our brand mission and the way we communicate with our customers and clients.

Another reason entrepreneurs fail is because the startup stage involves a lot of changes and evolving practices en route to finding a niche. Innovation and evolution is critical to keeping your business relevant and fresh, but there is a point where we need to stop changing every little detail and allow our businesses to naturally grow and bloom. We often allude to startups as newborn babies. It's a great analogy. We give both startups and babies round the clock attention, sacrificing on sleep and friendships and doing what we must to make it happen. Hard work is essential in the startup stage. The problems typically occur when our business is adolescent and still we are molly coddling it and smothering it because it's our baby.

Just like a baby, businesses begin to grow and function of their own accord. We give them the basic nutrients and teach them the basic ways of the world and then allow the baby to express itself within careful boundaries. As the baby grows, it becomes more independent and can begin to take care of some of its basic needs. We allow mistakes to happen but are there to comfort, guide and correct, allowing our baby to learn from experiences. As entrepreneurs, we are stifling the breath from our businesses by continually treating them like babies and forgetting they can grow up and express themselves without us getting in the way. We often get in our own way and wind up limiting our growth in life and business by trying to be God in every little detail.

There are many reasons why entrepreneurs and businesses at all levels fail, and I'm sharing just a few here. My last, and most important, point on why startups fail is that far too many entrepreneurs think their business is about what they want. This line of thinking trips up many people. Often, our businesses and products reflect who we are. While your business should represent you and your personal brand, fundamentally your business isn't about you. It isn't about your ego. It isn't even about whether you think it's good or not. It's all about your customer. It's about solving a problem, appealing to your customer base and whether your client has a need for what you offer.

We get so tied up with showing off our awards and what we've achieved. There certainly is nothing wrong with having pride in your work. In fact, I am the first to show the world when I have done something of which I am proud, but it's about the overall impression the customer or client gets from what we offer. It makes no difference if you think you have the best web site if your customer says it sucks. If we make our product or service about the customer, we'll be in business a very long time. If, on the other hand, it's all about you (perhaps how much you love it while being in complete denial that others think it sucks), we will become deaf and remain in our own bubble unable to see the reality that lays in front of us.

It's hard to take criticism. Often, it takes a level of maturity and wisdom to give credence to what others say. Certainly, some criticism is not worth your time, but if it's constructive and offered in a respectful way, you'd be foolish not to listen. As entrepreneurs, we don't like being told what to do. That's why many of us launched our own businesses in the first place. If you can balance drive and self-reliance with teachability and are realistic about your strengths and weaknesses, you will go far.

CHAPTER 25

DIFFICULT CHOICES

"Respect yourself enough to walk away from anything that no longer serves you, grows you, or makes you happy."
– Robert Tew

Don't work with a client just because they are willing to pay for your services. I find it baffling, though I can see the temptation, to work with anyone willing to pay your fees. Many of my clients have a similar problem. They all have one or two clients that are simply hard work. They change requirements. They don't pay invoices. They're needy and constantly demanding time and energy. They leave you feeling frustrated and tired, which negatively impacts the more glorious, fun and genuine clients for whom you love to go the extra mile but simply don't have the capacity.

Cash flow is king to any business. But when we agree to work with absolutely anyone willing to pay for our services, it isn't the best decision. I won't work with everyone. I have clear behavioural and mindset indicators to determine if I'm willing to invest my time and energy into a person. My clients have to want to grow and embrace being comfortable with being uncomfortable. If sessions only are about stroking ego, it's impossible to grow. I need to work with people who demonstrate the hunger and tenacity to move beyond current levels of achievement, who are fun to be around and ooze the energy and desire to be greater than what they are. When I see a great opportunity to work with a trailblazer, I have the motivation to invest in that person while protecting my enthusiasm for other likeminded clients.

I challenge you to start building filters with whom you do and do not work. You can start this process by examining your own key values. Start by writing a few of your key values down, then start to write down key attributes or attitudes you admire and for which you have the utmost respect. When you get clear on what type of energy, character or mindset an individual has and marry those values with any prospective customer or client, it will protect you from working with just anyone. I want to give my very best to those who give a crap and take their own personal and professional journey seriously.

Sometimes, we have to walk away from problematic clients. This is not just for your own sanity but also to lift the standards you have for yourself. Customers and clients have to be at the forefront of your mind and business, but it's important to consider the cost of continuing to work with someone who drags you down, is not responsible with their own time or money and constantly keeps you waiting to fulfil commitments.

I encourage you to be ruthless in evaluating the clients and customers you currently have. Here are a few red flags of which to take notice. If you identify any of these behaviours, it may be time to cut that client loose.

- **Bad attitude.** There's nothing worse than working with someone who is rude or negative. You should eradicate these people from your business to protect your brand. Don't desperately hold onto clients who constantly show this poor quality. It's great when you're able to address these issues with them, and they begin to change their behaviour. You'll know which are this type of client because they'll immediately spring to mind as you read this. You owe it to yourself and your happiness to get rid of them.
- **Don't respect your time.** They constantly turn up late for appointments, cancel appointments at the last minute and aren't prepared with the action points you've set out for them. They don't see your value.
- **Delaying payment.** This is a poor way to honour a working relationship. If you are constantly having issues with a client not paying or meeting the financial requirements of a project, you must stop working for them until they have cleared their commitment. Do not buckle or back down. Your customer is paying for your time, the way you think and what you bring to

the table. They are paying for your skill. Walk away if they're not prepared to honour you for the talent you bring.

- **Unrealistic expectations.** This point is more for those who have a service-based business. We must measure and communicate our expectations and our commitments to our clients. When a client is constantly demanding more but isn't compensating you accordingly, you must speak up and communicate these issues immediately.
- **No chemistry.** This red flag is absolutely an essential pass-fail before I work with any potential client. They have to have the spirit and desire to be all they can be. They have to be hungry and either fed up with their current condition or hellbent on being the best they can be. There must be a rapport. In order for me to be an effective mentor, you have got to like and trust me. If there is no synergy, why on Earth are you doing business with them?
- **They want you to work for free.** People will try it on, try and convince you they should have mate's rates or for you to help them because they are just starting out. They will play the sob story. They will pull out the friend card. Friends who want your skill for nothing are not being respectful of your time or value. If you offer to help, that's your prerogative. When you know your value, you will stop giving discounts. It is equally true that when you know your value, you'll stop giving people your time and talent for nothing.

CHAPTER 26

SHORTCHANGED

*"When you choose your friends, don't be shortchanged
by choosing personality over character."*
– W. Somerset Maugham

Have you ever walked into a shop, paid for goods and headed to your car only to realise you weren't given the right change or were overcharged for a product? It's never pleasant to believe you've received something at the value of X but paid Y. It leaves you feeling shortchanged. Having 12 years of hospitality experience under my belt, I rarely like to pick fault with the industry, but a recent customer service experience underpins this whole chapter in a powerful way.

I recently was part of a stag doo (bachelor party). We'd committed to pay for a private function room at a fine dining establishment, and the set meal option on top of the private room fee wasn't cheap. The views were incredible and expectations were high. We all were suited, booted and excited for a great night celebrating the imminent marriage of one of our dear friends.

I think you know where the story is going. A lot went wrong that night. The basic expectation for any restaurant patron is to have all food come out together at the right temperature and with the correct utensils and condiments. I waited and waited for my starter long after others already had finished theirs. We were only a party of 18 and yet four of us had to wait for the starters more than 10 minutes after our friends already had finished theirs. After that, it took another hour for our main courses to arrive. Of the 14 steaks ordered at our table, eight of them arrived cold and missing sides. Nothing about the experience said fine dining.

I always am intrigued by people's decisions about how to correct an unhappy customer's grievances. Sometimes they get it right, and sometimes they get it wrong. We were all just hoping for a pleasant night out and, although they discounted our bill, it still fell way short of what we were thinking in terms of compensation for a very disappointing experience. We all felt shortchanged. I told them what I believed the experience was worth, and it fell way short of what they insisted we pay. It's not pleasant to feel shortchanged.

We can feel shortchanged in personal and professional relationships too. One of my favourite proverbs, "Don't cast your pearls before swine", is a great metaphor for not giving what's precious (like your heart) to someone or something that doesn't nurture and protect it. Taking something precious and dragging it through the mud articulates a sense of casting aside something of value— in the case of the proverb, a pearl to pigs. Pigs will eat anything you throw at them. I remember going to a farmyard once. I watched this pig eating a child's shoe. They really will eat anything. We must be thoughtful and diligent stewards of to whom we give our sense of value, purpose and time. Sometimes, we have been needlessly hurt because of the poor choices we have made. We have shared something with someone and they have not cared for it. A shoe shouldn't end up in a pig's belly, and a person's heart shouldn't be given to another who doesn't know how to care for it.

Some people aren't deserving of our time. We must do good to all. We must love and be respectful, but this shouldn't be to the detriment of your own self-love. People will try to take advantage of you and your kindness. When we feel shortchanged in relationships, it's a clear indicator the people in whom we're investing are not the ones we should be.

All relationships are established by a mutual sense of wanting to grow together through encouragement, inspiration and challenges. We owe it to ourselves to be wise in whom we open ourselves to share our hearts. Your heart is the most precious and beautiful gift you can entrust to someone. When that trust is betrayed, you feel shortchanged.

It's so important the people we allow into our lives have a positive influence. We need to assess with whom we spend our time and whether we need to disassociate ourselves with some people. Just because you've been friends for years, doesn't give a person the right to abuse you or be unappreciative. We're not looking for perfect friends here. We're looking for people who give the best of themselves and have a positive impact in our lives.

Look out for these warning signs to prevent you feeling shortchanged in your relationships:

- **Backstabbers.** It may not be that they pull you down but perhaps they pull others down, belittling or sowing negativity and doubt in everyone they meet. They may make fun of others (how someone looks or dresses). If they say things behind the backs of others, what might they say about you?
- **Gossipers.** Gossip can be so destructive. It spreads like wildfire, breaks down trust and spreads doubt. Further, it slurs character without giving that person an opportunity to defend themselves. We need to be prepared to tell someone to their face when we have a problem. Take the high road, and stop gossiping.
- **Negative Neds and Nancy's**. That critical defeatist attitude paralyses you and what you want to do. I never take time for people who are negative because I can't dwell there for long. It's toxic and cuts off your supply of energy and ability to solve problems. Most people are negative because of their own issues. They don't want people to succeed because they can't succeed themselves and feel threatened by your success. They only expose their own weakness and vulnerability by attempting to stifle your dreams and put you down. Eradicate these naysayers from your life.

- **Manipulators.** It's awful to feel the traps of someone trying to manipulate and control you just to get what they want. Manipulation is generally about a fear of rejection. I remember once when I was manipulating an old girlfriend. I used to encourage her not to spend time with other guys, to let me know what she was doing, to encourage her to spend more time with me, but the more I tried to control her, the more she struggled for freedom. I wasn't proud of my actions or behaviours but soon realised the reason I was doing it was because I was afraid of losing her. I had experienced rejection before in my life, so I wanted to control her and prevent her from hurting me. What I did, instead, was stifle her. I stopped her from growing and allowing trust to form in our relationship. The relationship ended. Upon reflection, I decided if I was ever going to trust anyone again, I needed to change my belief that everybody in my life would reject me and turn me away. Thankfully, over time and with God's healing I no longer need to hold any relationship in such a way.
- **Selfish.** Some people constantly are looking out for number one— themselves. These people never check in to see how you are and always wait for you to make the first move. They don't instigate a meet up. Relationships have to be a two-way street. We must take time to organise and establish bonds through various activities. Occasionally, we must think upon the needs of those closest to us and provide an act of service or kindness that helps them know they are important to us. The relationships that are most dear to me are with people who give generously into my life in thought and deed and to whom I reciprocate with the fullness of joy. Watch out for those who take and who believe the world consists only of them. They constantly complain and moan and seek attention. They only think about how they feel. Get these kinds of people out of your life.

When you're constantly feeling drained and tired in a relationship, it's time to move on. Take your good heart and your valuable time and invest it elsewhere. You should be serious enough about the people in your life to put your foot down and establish boundaries. There probably are plenty of people in your life who need your positivity and energy. If it's constantly being abused by unappreciative others (and possibly some pigs), then you need to make those hard choices for the sake of your heart and for the sake of those who really do need and appreciate you.

CHAPTER 27

SELF PROMOTION

*"I've said it before, and by gosh, I'll say it again—
don't be afraid to toot your own horn."*
—Emlyn Chand

Self promotion versus nobody knowing you exist is something with which I constantly am wrestling. I haven't cracked it. It is tough to find that sweet spot between promoting one's self with a megaphone and a more reserved approach.

All entrepreneurs struggle with this. On the one hand, if we don't tell anyone about what we do, people never will know who we are. Often, when we start out in the world of entrepreneurship, we are every facet of our business, handling a variety of duties and responsibilities. We are the accountant, marketer and networker. This typically continues until we're in a position to take the plunge and hire help. Even then, we often are the main drivers of our businesses.

I've been called a "one-man marketing machine," but my background isn't in marketing. I've learned by reading and watching successful marketers. If we take a step back and look at what others are doing, we can find successful habits that can be useful in our own businesses.

As you may have noticed on my social media accounts, when someone buys my book I ask for a picture of them holding it. It isn't enough for me to say my book is selling. Here is visual evidence. When a potential reader sees others buying it, they naturally want to see what the fuss is about. Let's be real here. When we do something well and believe we can help people, we all take pride in it. I make no apologies for promoting my books. Of course, I want them to be successful, but I also want to impact people and make a difference.

We always will get people who become jealous of our success. It's something with which we all have to come to terms. When we don't come to terms with jealousy, it can derail us. None of us are exempt from attracting both those who love who we are and what we are about and also the polar opposite— those who want to see us fail. On the odd occasion, I have had people who value my success and those who like to ridicule it. It's part and parcel of any entrepreneur's journey. We mustn't become discouraged in the face of adversity. Even those who do not like you have paid you a huge compliment by taking time out of their day to comment or even criticise. When people gripe and moan about you, it's purely because they are unhappy with themselves. If people don't like your work, your Tweets or product, then they don't have to read or use them.

I understand, on social media, we all have a perception of others, and I am sure people perceive me a few different ways. Those who know me in real life know (while I am not shy about my successes), my life is far from the Mark Sephton show. We all have bills to pay and often young mouths to feed. We have to hustle. We have to build products and services and then make content to share across multiple platforms. Most of us do not promote our businesses for our own ego or to make ourselves look good. We share our work to make a contribution to the lives and businesses of others.

Everyone needs to tell the world about who they are and what they do without fear of the haters, doubters and those who simply don't understand. We should be proud of our work and its associated value.

One thing that's helped me find balance is the ability to give back by supporting and promoting others in the midst of my own promotion. I love seeing clients flourish and achieve success. I want to support and encourage those around me because as we encourage, applaud and share the work of others, people also innately see our sincerity. Volunteering our time and energy is a great way to give back. I recently became the chairman of the Coventry

Church District League to help support other churches in using football to build relationships and encourage strong Christian values in the community. We all give our time and energy to create a positive environment where men can come together with a common goal, enjoy each other's company, stay healthy and compete in friendly matches. I give my time because I believe in the vision of using sport to have a positive impact on the community and on the men themselves.

I know many of us love to create. We all have our own way of doing things. Many of us have our own businesses, some of us volunteer our time and energy to projects or to other people. Whether we are building our business or giving of our time freely, we all need to communicate our messages in a way that inspires and informs others of who we are and the work we do. Marketing in it's purest form is to storytelling. We need to invest in knowledge that serves our audience in a greater way. With that in mind, I wanted to share some marketing actions points to really help you tell your story and share it with the world.

Marketing Action Points:

- Take time to research current breaking news to ensure what you share is timely, relevant and sensitive to your audience. The timing of self promotion is critical. If something significant has happened in the world (like a natural disaster), we need to be sensitive toward current events. If you write a Tweet or post about your new blog or book when something serious is happening, it is going to potentially damage your brand because you will look out of touch and disrespectful. So, before you Tweet or post on social media, carry out some due diligence
- Take time each day to market someone else's success, and they may well turn around and market yours
- Tell stories in different ways. Think about how best

to deliver content— words, graphics, images, videos. Allow your own personality and creativity to shine through

- Get real and personal with your audience, and show them your human side. Speak with them not just about business but about some of the things you like. This is the quickest way to build a rapport. Learn to be the accessible face of your business that oozes personality. Let people know you're thinking about them by asking how they are. In short, engage with your audience. Stop automating Tweets, and be present on your social media channels

CHAPTER 28

THE RIPPLE EFFECT

"In every day, there are 1,440 minutes. That means we have 1,440 daily opportunities to make a positive impact."
– Les Brown

We only get one shot at life. We don't get to start over again. So take today, look it in the eye and make decisions based on living life the best we can. As I age and grow, I increasingly am aware of the impact I have on those around me— my children, family, friends and community. Am I challenging people to be all they can be? Am I challenging myself to grow through pain, discomfort, frustration and unrest? I want my life to be about more than only me and my success. I want to impact people in a sincere and genuine way instead of being focused only on making a name for myself. What's the point in that if I turn away the person in need who is right next to me. I want to be a vessel for good. My life is way bigger than any potentially selfish ambitions. I'm calling on you to be intentional with your life and be the best version of yourself you can.

Choose not to settle but, instead, to improve and strengthen your skill and wisdom to serve those less fortunate. The power of your name and accumulation of wealth doesn't matter. In the end, it's the legacy we leave behind for our children and grandchildren that's important. Keeping this in mind often helps to overcome suffering because you know life isn't just about you but about making a bigger impact through self-discovery and growth beyond fears and limitations.

I pray this book will impact you and help guide your life from this point on. I hope it lights a shift inside you to navigate back to the journey you should be taking. It's fine to have a great big business and tons of money, but these things should genuinely and authentically help others.

Use your influence and abundance to pour into others. Not all of us are able to fully embrace the spirit of Mother Teresa and be a channel of blessing and good that echoes through the ages. However, Mother Teresa is a great model to do good even in the small choices we make each day. Whether holding open a door, walking an elderly person across the road or doing the weekly shopping for a neighbour, we're constantly confronted with ways we can do unto others. It's really about the heart's attitude and your ability to think of others as well as yourself. We live in a corrupt world and need leaders of strength and purpose to equip each new generation. To be successful in this, we must stop being so passive, ward off procrastination and fear and get serious about our lives.

In a world filled with terrorism and disrespect for life, we must nurture life and take care of our fellow man. I regularly challenge myself in this way too. I sow seeds of good, but I can do more. You can do more too. We are better together. How is your life impacting others for the greater good?

We make the biggest impact when we know who we are deep down. When we protect and nurture our mind, we invest in key relationships, ask the hard-hitting questions and begin to define what we want our lives to look like and for what we want to be remembered. It's through honest reflection we find our own road map. There's nothing more infectious than when someone knows who they are and it oozes out of them. Be your own champion, and you'll pour out all that's good within you. When things don't go to plan, shout "Plot Twist" as loud as you can to find a fresh perspective and embrace the spirit of adventure.

Some of the greatest things I've done with my life so far came from left field and took me on a different path. I'm so thankful they did. Keep your eyes open, keep your mind active and be adaptable. Thinking on your feet and ridding yourself of frustration when things don't go to plan is the key to a happy and productive life. Here's to your success and impact on this world. We need more positivity warriors— those who do good, never sacrificing their beliefs for anyone or anything. It's when we embrace ourselves that we make the greatest impact on those around us. Now, go share your story and let your life ripple through eternity.

CHAPTER 29

THE WAY

"You don't choose a life, you live one."
– From the film: The Way

As you all know, I'm an avid film buff. A few years ago, I saw a film that really spoke to me at a time I needed to be uplifted. The 2010 film was Emilio Estevez's *The Way*. Dedicated to a traditional pilgrimage called the Camino de Santiago, *The Way* focuses on the love of the human spirit and chronicles a heartbroken father (played by Martin Sheen) who posthumously carries out what his late son had so longed to do. I now want to walk the Camino so I can have a deeper revelation of who I am as a person and what my life is all about.

The whole reason Estevez's character, Daniel, goes on the pilgrimage is to find himself. Many people go to the grave never knowing who they truly are because they've taken the road they believed others wanted them to take. Daniel didn't seem to measure up to his father's expectations, and this voyage really was about finding himself and getting some clarity. Sadly, Daniel's voyage was cut short when he was caught in a natural disaster and passed away.

Daniel's father, Tom, (played by Sheen) flies to France to collect his son's ashes and decides to complete the pilgrimage himself. Interestingly, so many people walk the Camino for so many varying reasons, and this is well demonstrated in the film. Tom, who was an eye doctor and seemed to have it all together back home in the United States, was the most lost out of them all. During the walk, he faced his own demons, failings and insecurities.

I repeatedly am inspired that Tom walked the Camino with his son's ashes, actually fulfilling the desire of his son. While Tom sets out thinking he'll complete the Camino to pay respect to his son, he actually ends up finding himself. Like so many of us today, Tom was focused on his work. Like many of my parent's generation, he was practical and wanted his children to have a job and play it safe. The

Camino opened Tom's eyes that life is about more than a job and money. Tom never had a great relationship with his son, but after the trek he found peace and oneness with his son once again.

That was one of the reasons I loved the film so much. We are all frail in our own humanity and sometimes think we have it all together until something life-changing yanks our security from under our feet and we find out what really matters in life. We have, no doubt, all experienced that sensation of walking through life unaware before getting a sharp metaphorical slap in the face that really determines of what you are made. This is the poetic story this film depicts. Walking around in a zombie state before embarking on a journey of self-discovery that cuts through our souls and enlightens us to our true purpose.

If you have never watched the film, I encourage you to do so. I really want to walk the Camino. The idea of walking and journeying to really find your way, your why and your purpose is powerful. I love that so many people of every ethnicity, religion and culture walk this path for varying reasons every year— from the spiritual to the practical. The film is an emotional one, but it's very relatable. Each time I watch it again, I see something different that speaks to my heart.

One of my long-time favourite scenes from the movie is when Tim and Daniel (father and son) talk about purpose. Tom strongly is directing his son to go to university, but Daniel is quick to correct his father by saying, "You don't choose a life, you live one." We all must make our own choices. We have to make our own beds and lie in them. While our parents or loved ones will always say what they sincerely believe we should do, we must first and foremost make our own decisions. I love that Daniel had the courage, despite not having his father's blessing, to pursue the life he wanted. That takes real guts and courage. We all want the support of those we love but, in some cases, it's important to follow your heart.

I lost a friend myself a few years ago. The one thing that gives me comfort in his loss is that he too died doing what he loved. He lived his life on his own terms. We all should strive to pass onto the next life doing what we love and living a life that is true to ourselves— even if those who love you have very different plans or aspirations.

We have so many people who come into our lives— some for seasons and some for life. As on the Camino, we all make an impact and leave an impression on each other. What a pilgrimage of this kind unveils is the beauty of searching the deepest parts of our hearts and minds while maintaining a collective togetherness that unlocks powerful secrets within us all. In this movie, the key was in the characters' abilities to communicate, be friends and go through an experience together, coming out the other side better for it. It is a beautiful movie and, as usual, it taught me a few things.

Which way are you going in life? Do you know your purpose (what you were put on Earth to do)? If not, you must set off on a pilgrimage of self discovery. It wasn't until I was 27 years of age that I really understood what I was put here to do. I am now on my own pilgrimage of creating the life I believe I was called to live. As Daniel said, "We don't choose a life, we live one." Live each day like it's your last and as though you're creating memories and legacies to leave behind for those you love.

CHAPTER 30

INDEPENDENCE

"The boat only rocks when people panic."
– Jason Vale

I love change. It's necessary to keep things fresh and evolving. The one thing I've been sharing through the past few weeks is the need for each of us to make our own choices based on what we believe is best for ourselves and our families. At times, we find ourselves involved in the world's uncertainties. For example, when the U.K. decided to leave the E.U. it struck fear and uncertainty into many and caused plenty of unrest and lots of questions. Donald Trump claiming the President Elect spot in the United States has raised a few eyebrows and will, of course, throw up plenty of debate, arguments and concerns.

However, in light of these events (and as entrepreneurs), we have an opportunity to find peace and success amongst the chaos. At the end of the day, we have contradictory feelings and fears we face regularly, but we can control these thoughts. We are in control of what we think, and it's our thoughts that are in a fight.

As entrepreneurs, we can affect and create our own economy even though we are part of something much bigger than ourselves. I don't mean to be naive when I say we create our own economy but, as entrepreneurs, if we bring something of value to market and we provide a solution to a problem, in many cases it doesn't always matter who is in power. Sometimes, the economy in which we find ourselves is volatile. During these times, we must look to pivot and evolve rather than accepting the perceived poor economy and using it as an excuse to give up.

Entrepreneurs are resilient, self-reliant, problem-solving and creative. We must take ownership of our own development— the ideas we bring into being and with which we take action. For those of us who live in the entrepreneurial revolution of self creation, we have built a lifestyle that isn't dependent on going to school or a guaranteed job and retiring with a gold watch at 65. That is the industrial revolution— a conveyor belt of production. Brexit meant business as usual for me. It didn't change my drive to create and innovate without excuses.

How often in life do we go through uncertainty? Life is full of risks and, for many, this is uncomfortable and maybe even painful. When uncertainty and fear come to our door, we need to circle the wagons and come together. We can't resist anymore. We have to work with what we have.

Changing the way you see things:

- **Look for the positives.** Edison never focused on the failing but looked at the knowledge gained from each failure. Each failing taught him a lesson and revealed some new insight or strategy. If we are going to change the way we look at things, we have to see the opportunities and not the obstacles.
- **Confront things in the opposite spirit.** If you want to lose weight, don't think of it as depriving yourself of certain foods or how tiring exercise will be. Think about the good, nutritional foods you can eat and how fabulous you will look and feel after periods of exercise. Allow uncertainty to lead you to hope, curiosity and self discovery.
- **Get understanding.** When we enquire, explore and make the effort to understand an individual or a situation, it gives us a clearer understanding of the motivations to push for change or the way someone reacts to a problem. Sometimes I scratch my head why people make the decisions they do, but when I enquire and am informed I can begin to understand why they reacted or behaved in a certain way even when I disagree or disapprove.
- **Remain teachable.** If we want to grow, we have to admit we don't know everything. We don't know what we don't know. It isn't until new revelations are made

that we alter our viewpoint or belief system. If we are so pigheaded and stubborn (there is a place to be both of those things), we will never grow, adapt and change. I once was a judge for the Royal Bank Of Scotland, issuing grants to nonprofits and enterprises. As a judge, we had to rank each proposal and then come together as a group to deliberate which nonprofit should receive a grant. Our varying experiences and wisdom impacted on our final decisions, but it was our ability to remain objective and consider the other views around the table that led to a group decision.

- **Don't look back.** The only time we should look back is when we are considering where we came from on our journey to self discovery. Of course, our history can be a great tool for future decisions. However, we must be consistent looking toward creating new paths for our lives rather than trying to go back to a place in our life when things seemed more rosy. When we sign up to a gym membership in January in line with our New Year's resolutions and find ourselves watching Netflix by March, we beat ourselves up for our lack of self control and falling into bad habits. We need to keep looking ahead and play the long game. We need to stay consistent and not allow our emotions to make up our minds while continually doing what is right over what is easy. I have talked about environments and the need to surround yourself with positive people who help to build accountability and keep you from falling back to the place where you started. Keeping looking forward. Where our eyes focus, so our legs will follow.

CHAPTER 31

PERSONAL DEVELOPMENT

"Treat a man as he is and he will remain as he is. Treat a man as he can and should be and he will become as he can and should be."
– Stephen Covey

Many people ask where my personal development journey began. It's a great question. It makes me smile, as I believe this journey became the very catalyst to fire me on a path of excitement and adventure. When we develop our mind, attitude, skill, ability, thoughts and strategies, we naturally improve on the impact, influence, credibility and reputation people glean from us.

Developing myself has resulted in far more opportunities than I ever could have imagined. The greatest place to invest is in yourself. There is no better place than that. Since that revelation many years ago at Dani Johnson's First Steps to Success seminar (more on that in *Inside Job*), I consistently have invested in myself. I have been focused, meticulous and religious in improving my craft, focusing on the core of my strengths and abilities.

There always will be room to grow and expand beyond my current successes and limitations. Personal development is a lifelong journey of commitment, pain, breakthrough and personal revelation. I find it staggering that the more I learn the less I actually know. It's so exciting to know that 12 months ago I didn't operate at the level I do now. The encouragement there is that, in another 12 months time, I shall be operating at another increased level in line with my personal development. Each year, I set the goals, habits and behaviours to track in order to wind up at a better place. By better, I mean more enlightened and operating with greater knowledge and influence. I can see problems before they arise. I can pivot and innovate.

Personal development started with the soul-searching question, "What do I want to do with my life?" I began thinking about where I was and what, indeed, I was doing with my life. At the time, I was working in hospitality, hustling amongst branded and unbranded restaurants.

I was good at hospitality. While certain elements of the industry allowed me to flex my skills and passions, I knew my desire to positively influence people was better served in other ways. That revelation set me on a path to develop the skills and influence I already had exhibited but never honed. I embarked on leadership, business and life coaching training to develop my natural ability to lead. Once I had determined what I wanted out of life, I could make choices that were inline with that vision. My desire to help people opened doors and led me to my current path. Since that time, my desire to help others only has increased and keeps me hungry to continue my quest for personal development.

Not only do we need to find what we want out of life, but we have to become a master of it. We all have skills and strengths. The sweet spot is marrying your passion and your skill. This is where you become naturally motivated to invest the time and devotion to develop yourself and create opportunities.

It really helps your personal development when you are confident in who you are. This is how you become a master. Are you ready for any opportunity that comes your way and is inline with your life's purpose and mission? In order to invest valuable time into personal development, we all have to like who we are and have the confidence and understanding to know we're worth it. Let's make something clear... I believe wholeheartedly that I am worth investing in, but I also believe you are worth investing in too. None of us invests in anything we can't get behind. None of us invests in a company we know is already doomed, and none of us are going to invest our time in a relationship we know is toxic and damaging. If you struggle in your own personal development, perhaps you don't recognise your own value. If that's the case, you need to find a mentor, coach or success buddy to help you process and journey through these self-limiting lies.

I invest in myself because I believe God has given me blueprints, skills, knowledge and strategies I may not have unearthed yet. If we were to rewind the clock on years gone by and you had the opportunity to invent Facebook or Apple or any other big invention, you would invest all your time and money and expertise into it because you knew without a shadow of a doubt it was going to make you stinking rich with huge amounts of influence. I guarantee that if you develop yourself (invest in you, your mind, your beliefs, your abilities), you will indeed reap a harvest of success, reward and influence.

We all need mentors and coaches. I have a success buddy with whom I meet regularly. I value this relationship so much because none of us can do life alone. We all need encouragement. We all need to be challenged, and we all need someone who is on the outside looking in. It's a place where I can go when I have messed up, when I am tired, discouraged, confused and perhaps angry and deflated. Even though I am super positive, there still are times when I just need to unload, unplug and share my unhappy thoughts in an environment that is safe and, maybe, uncomfortable. What I mean by uncomfortable is someone telling you what you need to hear rather than what you want to hear. We need, at least, one person in our lives to give it to us straight. My development demands it. We all can be quickly deceived by our own levels of success and become blindsided. In order to develop, I must know when to ask for help and from whom to ask it. Many of you have made the mistake of trusting and opening up to the wrong person. Please don't stop trusting and opening up. Just learn to be wise with whom you do it. That's the only difference. It's not healthy for you to be doing everything alone and living a life of solitude.

People often have said, "Mark, you are great at articulating your thoughts and feelings into words." It's true, that from a young age, I have listened to my heart and the way I feel. While that has been extremely painful at times, it has served me in my ability to develop myself. We need to be excellent communicators in order to establish boundaries and share how we think and feel for others to help us and respect our choices and wishes. Our ability to express how we think and feel is meaningful to forming collaborations. These deeper connections are key to ensuring our words and thoughts resonate with others. If we have a synergy and relate to one another, you are more likely to journey with me in a trusting way.

Our ability to develop how we communicate and, most importantly, how we feel will start to unlock relationships not just with our spouses or children but with our clients too.

I already have explored the need to be creative. I have banged the drum about the ways in which creativity reaches its peak when we are in a place of positivity and gratitude. We must find the culture to express and share our creative flair. We need more opportunities in life to allow our imaginative minds to create. As we are on this road of personal development, we need to find expression and the need to articulate our creative flair. I challenge you not to suppress your hunger to create but tap into it. Don't let others keep you contained. Let out who you are and what you were created to express in all its glory. When we express ourselves, that's when we develop internally and when people start to see who we really are.

I remember the first time I went on radio. I loved the concept and the idea. I spent about eight hours in a classroom covering all the technicalities of music faders, mic levels, editing, broadcasting and the like. I knew I was good at talking. I could talk to anyone, which is something for which I am very grateful to the hospitality industry. I had to talk to people and started to like talking to people.

We all know theory and classroom-based learning is no substitute for the real thing. Yes, I could talk, but could I control and manage the thousands of buttons in a radio studio. I did the best I could, which wasn't great but I never made any huge faux pas. The task at hand was new, and I wasn't going to ridicule myself while listening back to my first radio hosting experience.

You have to commend yourself and others for trying something for the first time. I now look back on five years of radio broadcasting and see the development and improvement to my ability to ask great questions and manage a desk with its thousands of faders and controls. I've even become adept at bringing it all together in seamless harmony. I still make mistakes and can't get lazy or take shortcuts because it shows. Your ability to try new things, progress and stick with something is the difference between success and failure. If we want to develop, we have to experience new things. We can then decide whether we are going to adopt it into our life and improve upon it.

I am always mindful of everything going on in my life— especially those difficult, hard and awkward times. I don't reflect on them to send me down a road of depression but to be fully aware in the hope that I can one day help others going through the same trials. It's helpful to walk a difficult or painful road and come out of the other side. This process allows us be more readily empathetic toward what others may be feeling in a given situation. The more aspects of life we experience, the more reliable and steadfast we can be for those around us.

In *Inside Job*, I talked about the importance of values. Each of us should have our own core values and beliefs as a framework for the way we live and how we conduct ourselves. When we are on this personal development journey, we must be aware of our values to ensure we don't change them when times get tough. When we know our own beliefs and values, we can then nurture and strengthen them to aid our development. If you find yourself compromising your values, it will not only unsettle you but cause miscommunication within your network. If you want to develop beyond where you are now, you must stay true to you. Even when the temptation is strong to give in or surrender to the pressure of others, you must resist.

Finally, the key we all must unlock is our ability to stay consistent and grounded when it comes to our emotions. We often allow the emotion surrounding an event to cloud or drive our decisions. Often, we are called to do what is right over what is easy. Have we developed an ability to harness our emotion in a way that doesn't cause harm to others or ourselves? Some people struggle to share emotions at all and others tend to find it hard not to show the world how they really feel. Feelings are important but can be selfish and result in flare ups of anger that only will cause further problems.

We need to nurture maturity in ourselves and not allow our emotions to get the better of us. We must seek to develop our understanding of how we feel and become wise in how we express ourselves. We all need to be responsible for our actions. We can't be governed by the adage, "If it feels good, do it." That line of thinking will get you into trouble because you fail to consider consequences. How much control do you have over yourself? If the honest answer is less than desirable, you may want to seek help to improve that and reduce the risk of self harm when your emotions run amuck.

FINAL THOUGHTS

"It's not where you start that matters. It's where you finish that counts."
– Zig Ziglar

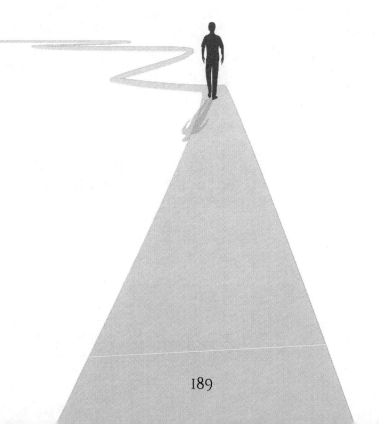

Regardless of our individual journeys, the one thing we all must do is finish our race strong. If you are reading this, it's not too late for you to change, improve or develop. Everything we go through in life (the plot twists, the straight, the narrow and the bumpy) is for our greater good. We can take the learnings, setbacks, confusion and uncertainty and apply them to finishing strong. We have seen some of the mightiest and strongest men and women fall at the last hurdle, as a poor choice or mistake costs them dear. Still, they stagger across the finish line. I don't want to go out with a whimper. I want to make sure I end this life strong and that who I am and the waves I created will continue to ripple through my children, their children and beyond.

For those who don't like surprises and read the last chapter first or those who just have short attention spans, here's everything you need to know about *Plot Twist* summed up in one neat and tidy list. I'm not saying don't read the book (you'll get more out of it that way), but this can serve as a roadmap for success.

Takeaways from each chapter:

Chapter 1 – Be intentional in all your relationships
Chapter 2 – Keep your eyes open and ears engaged; You don't know who you will meet
Chapter 3 – Be present in every moment
Chapter 4 – Take the initiative, and be the opportunity
Chapter 5 – Give all you have to everything you do
Chapter 6 – We rarely get a second opportunity to make a long-lasting impression
Chapter 7 – We can achieve more together
Chapter 8 – Knowing who you are is the most exciting place to be
Chapter 9 – Create accountability in your life; It will protect you and help you grow

Remember, when things don't go to plan, shout, "Plot twist" and allow the energy of adventure and uncertainty to excite you and ignite your curiosity!

Please leave an honest review on Amazon and Goodreads. Thank You :-)

THANK YOU

Thank you...

... to all the people I've had the good fortune to meet in recent years. I've met some truly inspiring people, and I hope you know who you are. As always, my gratitude is overflowing to my family for their ongoing love, support and encouragement and to my church and pastors for their wisdom, support and prayers. I also want to say "thank you" to Heather Westbrook for honouring me with her creative flair in delivering another kick ass book design and graphics, as well as to my editor, Meredith Pruden, for her high standards and for pushing me to limits I wasn't even sure I could reach. To all the doubters, naysayers and trolls, thank you for your criticism. Not only do I often get a kick out of it, but it really does drive me forward. Last, but certainly not least, thank you to my personal Lord and Saviour, Jesus Christ, for always lifting me up in times of need.

Plot Twist is dedicated to the life of Andrew Wolfindale. Andrew was a son, a brother and a friend to many, and he was a shining example of living your life to its fullest potential and with purpose. You'll always be in our hearts, Andrew. We'll see you soon.

Also by

MARK SEPHTON

Discover. Imagine. Achieve.

MARK SEPHTON

DISCOVER who you are.
IMAGINE who you could be.
ACHIEVE all the potential within you.

MARK SEPHTON is an international mentor to entrepreneurs whose inaugural book *Inside Job* debuted in 2014. In addition to mentoring and writing, Mark also hosts a radio show, *Talk Business* on Radio Plus Coventry, where he expresses his love for entrepreneurship and provides expert guidance to entrepreneurs each Wednesday. Mark is a regular contributor to *Entrepreneur* magazine online, and has spoken on numerous business stages worldwide. An advocate of living your truth, Mark is a master of evolving life experiences into successful businesses that draw out the magnificent potential each of us hold.

WWW.MARKSEPHTON.COM

94332343R00109

Made in the USA
Columbia, SC
30 April 2018